Jim Valvano's
Guide to
Great Eating

ALSO BY JIM VALVANO

**Too Soon to Quit: The Story of N.C. State's
1983 National Championship Season**

Jim Valvano's Guide to Great Eating

Edited by Robert W. McDowell and Anne B. George

Illustrated by Jackie Pittman

PUBLISHED BY JTV ENTERPRISES, CARY, N.C.

1984

ACKNOWLEDGMENTS

First, I would like to thank all the restaurants, relatives, friends — and friends of friends — who have shared secrets from their kitchens. Without their generosity, there would be no book.

Second, I would like to express my gratitude to my parents and wife, for their countless contributions and suggestions. This cookbook simply could not have been compiled without the very active assistance of Rocco and Angelina Valvano, who personally contacted dozens of family members and old family friends concerning this project; or without the help of my wife Pam, who wrote and/or telephoned numerous friends we made during my basketball coaching career.

Third, many thanks are also due to the members of the cookbook's production team (listed below), whose combined talents have made this a book of which we can all be proud; to my business manager, Dick Stewart, who handled the day-to-day details of this project; and to Wolfpack basketball secretary Frances Lewis, who fielded a million messages and kept us all straight about who was supposed to do what when.

Finally, I would like to acknowledge special debts to Anne George, who not only edited and organized the recipes initially in hand, but also was instrumental in obtaining many overdue items and a number of new recipes as well; to Carol Hall, who served as unofficial consultant for the "Tailgating Treats" section; to the Wolfpack Club's Jimmy Bass, whose knowledge of North Carolina's culinary treasures is extraordinary; to *Too Soon to Quit* Editor and Publisher Stuart Coman, who contributed valuable marketing advice; to Jean Hall of Hunter Publishing Company, Inc., who displayed limitless patience in this, her second, project with this author; and to Sisters' Garden of Eating and North Ridge Country Club — both of Raleigh — which, on very short notice, each loaned me complete chef's outfits, parts of which can be seen in the photo on the back cover.

PRODUCTION TEAM

Project Manager/Editorial Coordinator . . . . Robert W. McDowell
Editorial Consultant . . . . Judy Bolch
Production/Marketing Coordinator . . . . Stuart George Communications
Associate Editor . . . . Anne B. George
Cover Design/Illustrations . . . . Jackie Pittman
Graphic Design and Layout . . . . Donna Robinson
Typography . . . . Glenn Godfrey Communications, Inc.
Photography . . . . Greg Gibson
Color Separations . . . . Watkins Color Graphics, Inc., Southern Pines, N.C.
Printer . . . . Hunter Publishing Company, Inc., Winston-Salem, N.C.

PREFACE

Call me the Will Rogers of eating. I never met a meal I didn't like.

I come by that naturally. My wife Pam put it best when she said my family doesn't eat to live, we live to eat.

You're talking about a guy who went into the food business for himself when he was eight or nine years old. I broke in with things called *fritta é mangia* — "fry and eat."

You made some pizza dough; you dropped it by spoonfuls into very hot oil and, after frying, drained the little balls on paper towels; then you rolled them in powdered or granulated sugar. I'd take them out on the corner and sell them. Usually I'd gobble up so many that I'd eat up the profits. Ray Kroc, I wasn't.

You're talking about a family that had Aunt Marion. One Christmas Aunt Marion, who lived right across the street from us in Queens, N.Y., started over with a pan of her famous homemade lasagne. It was an icy day, and before she knew it, Aunt Marion's feet had slipped out from under her. Did she drop the pan and put out her hands to catch herself? Nope.

Like any true lover of Italian food, Aunt Marion clung to the pan and slid on down the street. We finally rescued her and the lasagne. She was a little wet, but the lasagne had never touched the ground.

It's memories like those that made me want to write this cookbook.

Aunt Marion's recipes and those of the other people in my family are an important part of my heritage. When I think of what we ate together, I think of the people and the love we shared. Aunt Marion is gone now, and many of her dishes can never be recreated. But I wanted to keep the legacy of Aunt Marion and all my relatives for my children. I wanted to share what they meant to me. I wanted to write it all down so that the meals and the joy wouldn't be forgotten.

It's Italian food, of course, that I grew up with. But over the years, my wife's cooking and my friends' cooking and the meals I've had in restaurants have all enriched my life. I've learned to like brisket and barbecue as well as braciola. So I wanted to include those kinds of recipes in the book, too.

Maybe I better mention one thing, just so I won't be accused of not following the truth-in-advertising rules. I do not like liver. I will not eat liver. I do not include any liver recipes in this book.

I bet that even Will Rogers didn't like liver.

Some of the recipes are strictly sentimental. Some are gourmet. They come from friends all over the United States, from my family and from restaurants. All are good eating. And any average cook could, I think, prepare them with the directions I've given.

I just hope that when you try one of the recipes, you'll get a little taste of what it meant to me.

Enjoy.

CONTENTS

Just an Italian Kid from Queens

My first cravings were for marshmallow cookies—you know, the ones with two wafers and a marshmallow in the middle. Maybe Freud would say that signifies what a nice guy I am at heart or something. Probably what it shows is how early I learned to appreciate food.

Food's always been one of my life's primary ruling forces. My mother claims she never had any difficulty getting me to eat—but, boy, was it hard to make me stop.

When my brothers Nick and Bobby and I went out to play in the street, we'd ask my father how far we could go. He'd say, "If you can't hear me whistle, you're too far." What he'd be whistling for, of course, was to call us home for a meal.

Our neighborhood—the Corona section of Queens, N.Y.—was all Italian. We'd always have a couple of kids who had just come over from Italy, and being the good young fellows that we were, we would try to help out the new arrivals. Like showing them, for example, that nickels, being bigger than dimes, certainly were worth more. We were always willing to exchange as many nickels as they would like for dimes. Just being neighborly, you understand.

That was the kind of stuff we were up to, so probably the only thing that kept us honest was that mealtime came around often enough to interfere with our bigger schemes.

One of my favorite meals was a gravy sandwich. The "gravy" was really tomato sauce. But we called it a gravy sandwich—oregano and sauce and braciola (flank steak), on Italian bread—and it was great.

Just buying the bread was a treat. You'd go to the local bakery and get these long loaves and take them home sticking out of a brown paper bag. Before you got home, you'd eat the ends off, and they were hot and delicious.

Then there was the lemon ice we loved. That was an Italian ice that at first only came in a lemon flavor. When we'd ask for it, we said it so fast that it came out "lemonice."

Then Nick, the Lemon Ice King of Corona, started making the ice in all flavors. We still called them all "lemonice."

You'd get chocolate lemonice or strawberry lemonice. For a dime, you could get a double scoop with chocolate syrup on it.

The big meal of the week came every Sunday at 2. It was almost always Italian. (But we ate American too sometimes.) My favorite Sunday dinner was ravioli with cheese. Mama would make the pasta herself. (Sometimes she let me make the shells if she was serving manicotti.)

Before dinner we'd go to church. My brother Nick was an altar boy, and we'd go watch him serve Mass. I was also studying to be an altar boy, but I was unceremoniously dismissed because I talked too much. I could never shut up. I was always disturbing the class, so finally they asked me to go into something else.

After Sunday dinner, we'd go over to my grandfathers'. I'm named after my Mom's dad, but I look like my father's dad. My brother Nick's named after my father's father, and he looks like my mother's father. My parents sure fouled up that one.

When I think back to the happiness of my childhood, I realize we didn't have a whole lot of material things. But we had something that we don't have now. Every night we sat down to dinner together—all five of us.

We didn't have to worry about getting everyone together on March 10 for my birthday, because when March 10 came, it was not going to be that much different from March 9 or March 11. We were together March 10 and we were going to be together March 9 and March 11. Every day we were together for dinner at 6 o'clock.

The thing that I remember the most was love. It was a constant. If I had to pick one single word to describe my whole childhood, growing up first in Queens and later in Seaford, Long Island, it would be that word — love.

And the food expressed that love. I could come home and say, "Mom, I'm dying for some escarole soup." Snap. And it's done. I could call up from college and bring the whole floor of my dorm home for an Italian meal.

I blame my wife for making my mother retire from being an Italian mother. She retired, somewhere along the line, and became an American mother. Which means that if you call up and say you're bringing six people home for dinner, she says, "Fine. Stop on the way and grab some food."

In this chapter, I include a holiday meal like the one my Mama used to make. She'd serve antipasto, prosciutto and melon, manicotti with her own special meat sauce (three kinds of meat), a roast meat, baked sweet potatoes, tossed salad, fresh vegetables and cream puffs.

Now most of us would consider that a pretty good spread. And it was. But that was what Mama had when she cooked it all and invited over the family.

On a REALLY big holiday — Christmas or Easter, say — the meal was even more of a production. You're talking about starting to eat at about 1 or 2 o'clock and you're going to midnight, babe. You're looking at a 10-hour affair.

Everybody would bring a special dish.

You'd start with the antipasto — cheese, bread, sausage, pickles, cold cuts, stuffed mushrooms, stuffed artichokes, artichoke hearts, celery with special dips, different beans and salads. All that.

To be honest with you, a lot of the men didn't like the antipasto. It was mostly the aunts; it was aunts' food. The thing I remember most was the big green olives and sucking the pimiento out. As a kid, that's got to be one of the most fun things in the world. You'd sit there and while everybody else was into anchovies and special little fish things, you're taking the green olives and — slurp — getting those pimientos out and all the while hearing the adults talk about how olives make you sexy. (And I'm thinking, "How many can I eat without losing control?")

Remember this is the prelude to what's coming...the anti-pasta before the pasta.

Then you had your wine, your little before-dinner wine from a jug, a great big jug of dago red.

You'd probably eat a good 45 minutes. Then you'd take a little break.

And I remember the blessing before the meal. It was always special to see who was going to be asked to say grace. You know me and my big mouth. I used to say it a lot. I liked to say it.

Then you'd go to the soup.

If this were Christmas or New Year's Day, the men would be watching the football games or maybe shooting pool. (Everybody always had pool tables.) And the women were making dinner. (Remember, the women didn't *allow* the men in the kitchen where we could get in the way.)

Then they'd call us to the table for the first course. Sometimes we'd eat American first, and then Italian. If it was Thanksgiving, we always had ham and turkey—not one, but both. And with that, you always had sweet potato soufflé with marshmallow topping, regular sweet potatoes AND regular baked potatoes.

We always had corn, too, and three or four different vegetables and applesauce. We'd eat all that. Now the next bottle of wine came out for the next part of the meal, and we'd eat all that.

Then we'd take another break.

Then we'd come back and eat ITALIAN. We would usually have two types of pasta. Maybe manicotti—it's like a pancake rolled up with ricotta cheese inside. We might have lasagne or ravioli. With that you'd have Italian bread and a glass of wine.

Then after you ate THAT, you'd bring out all the meat, the meatballs and the pork and the braciola and the sausage.

Then we'd have Italian pastries and chestnuts and big baskets of fruits.

And about 7 at night, you'd start in again. They'd say "Do you want the Italian or do you want the American?" And they'd bring it all out again. That's how you'd go to 10 o'clock.

When you think about it, it's really shocking, isn't it?

We had a family big enough to take care of a lot of food, though. My father's father built the homes that we all lived in. He had six children. We all lived right there in Corona—except for Aunt Rosie, who lived in Butte, Montana. How that happened, we never knew. Maybe she moved to get away from the subway. Our house was right under the El.

Like most Italians, my parents came from big families. The son of Nicholas and Vita (Cava) Valvano—originally from Naples, Italy—my father was named Rocco, but has been called "Rocky" most of his life. He had two brothers—Thomas and Bruno—and three sisters—Philomena (DiPierro), Rose (Orrino) and Marion (Anselmo).

My mother's maiden name is Angela Vitale—but I have always called her "Angelina," in the Italian manner; she's come to accept it; and that's the way her name appears in this book. Her parents, James and Mary (Liano) Vitale, had one son—Nicholas—and four other daughters—Josephine (Ricco), Helen (Tassani), Rosemary (Mesiti) and Annette (Celano).

Of course, when my brothers Bobby and Nick and I were little, we couldn't pronounce the names of my mother's sisters, so we ended up calling them "Auntie Josie," "Auntie Hel," "Auntie Roro" and "Auntie Na"—and still do to this day. And my cousins still call my Mom "Auntie Gigi."

When we were all growing up together in Corona, whenever we cousins wanted to do something we were not allowed to do at home, we could always go over to the house of my Aunt Marion, who, perhaps because she had no children of her own, treated us all like *her* children.

Once I watched a "Mr. Wizard" show in which he told you how to take an egg and boil it in vinegar to make a rubber egg you could bounce.

My mother said, "Not here, you're not going to make them." So zip, we went over to Aunt Marion's. We boiled eggs in vinegar all day and stunk up her house and bounced the eggs all over the place.

She was also the first woman I knew to have all different flavors of soda pop in her refrigerator. She was wonderful. She let me have a different can of soda with ice cream for breakfast each day—the couple of months I lived with her while my family was moving out to Seaford, Long Island, the year I was 13.

Your mother would *never* let you have soda and ice cream for breakfast. And I don't recommend it. But it's great when you're 13 years old, I'll tell you that.

In the pages that follow, you'll find my Mom's recipes for a complete holiday dinner like she'd prepare at home and when the whole family wasn't getting together for a *major* holiday like Thanksgiving, Christmas, New Year's or Easter. This dinner is followed by a generous sampling of "family favorites" each relative might bring when the Valvano or Vitale clans assembled en masse for an afternoon and evening of *serious* eating.

MAMA VALVANO'S HOLIDAY MEAL

Antipasto
Prosciutto and Melon
Manicotti with Meat Sauce
Roast Meat
Baked Sweet Potatoes
Tossed Salad
Fresh Vegetables, Italian Style
Cream Puffs with Italian-Style Filling

ANTIPASTO

1 head iceberg lettuce, shredded
6 slices Genoa salami
6 very thin slices prosciutto
4 celery hearts, cut in half
lengthwise
½ cup pickled eggplant
8 green olives
8 black olives
6 marinated artichoke hearts
1 small jar or can of pimientos
½ pound mozzarella cheese,
sliced
½ pound provolone, sliced
Vinegar and oil dressing

Use large oval platter. Cover platter with bed of shredded lettuce. Mound center with cheeses. Arrange rest of ingredients around mound, making an attractive design.

PROSCIUTTO & MELON

Cut chilled cantaloupe, honeydew or Persian melon lengthwise in half and remove seeds and rind.

Cut fruit into crescent-shaped slices and put 1 or 2 on each serving plate. Cover each melon slice with thin slices of prosciutto and garnish with a thin wedge of lime.

MANICOTTI

CREPES

1 cup flour
1 cup water
1 teaspoon baking powder
2 eggs, beaten
Pinch of salt

Mix all ingredients. Grease and preheat 6-inch frying pan. Pan need only be greased once. Drop ¼ cup of batter into pan, tilting pan to cover surface. When set on one side, flip over and let other side set. Do not brown crepes. Set aside. Prepare filling.

FILLING

1½ pounds ricotta cheese
½ pound mozzarella cheese, cubed or grated
½ cup Romano cheese, grated
Salt and pepper
1 tablespoon parsley, chopped

Blend all ingredients together. Spread a tablespoon or two of filling on each crepe, roll and close. Place filled manicotti, seams side down, side by side in a baking dish and cover with Meat Sauce and grated cheese.

Bake in preheated 350-degree oven 15 minutes.

MEAT SAUCE

SAUCE

¼ cup olive oil
1 medium onion, chopped
2 cloves garlic, minced
2 (28-ounce) cans crushed tomatoes
2 (6-ounce) cans tomato paste
1 bay leaf
1 teaspoon basil, crushed
1 teaspoon salt
Dash of pepper
2 cups water

Heat oil in large frying pan. Sauté onion and garlic until tender. Add tomato paste. Simmer 2 minutes. Add tomatoes. Blend tomatoes if you prefer them puréed. Add water and bring to a boil. Add bay leaf, basil, salt and pepper. Add all the meat which has been browned separately, including the oil and scrapings from the frying pan. Cover tightly. Simmer 2 hours, stirring every 15-20 minutes.

BRACIOLA

2 thin slices (6 inches by
6 inches) round steak
Romano cheese, grated
Parsley, chopped
Garlic, minced
Salt and pepper
¼ cup olive oil

Sprinkle each slice of steak generously with cheese, parsley and garlic. Season to taste with salt and pepper. Roll each slice separately and secure with a string or toothpicks. Brown well in oil. Add to the sauce with sausages and meatballs.

SAUSAGES

6 links sweet Italian sausage
2 links hot Italian sausage
(optional)

Prick sausages before frying. Brown in oil in a frying pan. Add to the sauce with braciola and meatballs.

MEATBALLS

1 pound ground chuck
½ pound ground pork
¼ cup Romano cheese, grated
1 tablespoon parsley,
finely chopped
2 eggs
½ teaspoon salt
⅛ teaspoon pepper
1 clove garlic, minced
3 slices of bread

Remove crust from bread, soak bread in water and squeeze dry. Place all ingredients in a bowl and mix thoroughly. Shape into balls. Brown well and add to sauce with sausages and braciola.

NOTE:
Mama Valvano's Meat Sauce may also be served with lasagne, ravioli or spaghetti. Meat Sauce recipe is adequate for 2 pounds of spaghetti.

ROAST MEAT

The meat served with the meal depends on which holiday we are celebrating. We have roast turkey at Thanksgiving, ham at Christmas and lamb at Easter. For other holiday dinners, we have roast beef.

BAKED SWEET POTATOES

Wash and scrub sweet potatoes. (The amount depends on the size of the potatoes and the appetites of individual diners.) Then dry and grease lightly with butter. Bake in preheated 425-degree oven for 40-60 minutes, depending on the size. When potatoes are half done, puncture skin once with fork, permiting steam to escape to prevent bursting. Return to oven and finish baking. Potatoes are done when a fork slides easily into the potato flesh.

TOSSED SALAD

With the meal, we serve a mixed green salad of cucumbers, lettuce, tomatoes and sweet red onions tossed with oil and vinegar.

FRESH VEGETABLES, ITALIAN STYLE

The vegetable varies, but usually we have green beans or broccoli or cauliflower, prepared Italian style. This means the vegetable is cooked by steaming or boiling. Then garlic is sautéed in olive oil and the cooked vegetable is tossed with the flavored oil.

CREAM PUFFS

MAKES 16-20

½ cup butter
1 cup water
1 cup flour
Dash of salt
4 eggs

Place butter, water and salt in saucepan. Bring to a boil. Add flour all at once. Stir vigorously until mixture leaves the sides of the pan.

Remove from heat and add eggs, one at a time, beating after each egg is added. Drop by teaspoons on ungreased shallow pan.

Bake in preheated 425-degree oven 20 minutes. Reduce heat to 375 degrees and bake 20 minutes more or until golden brown and cooked through. Remove and let cool on a rack. May be filled with heavy cream, whipped and sweetened, or Italian-style filling.

ITALIAN-STYLE FILLING

1 pound ricotta cheese, well drained
½ square chocolate, grated
1 teaspoon almond extract
1 tablespoon citron, grated
3 tablespoons milk

Blend all ingredients thoroughly. Add milk sparingly to achieve custard-like mixture. Fill puffs.

APPETIZERS

BATTER-DIPPED CAULIFLORETS

1 head cauliflower, separated into florets
2 eggs, beaten
1 tablespoon cheese, grated
1 tablespoon parsley, chopped
½ cup flour
6 tablespoons oil
Salt and pepper to taste

Parboil florets, but do not overcook. Drain.

Add cheese, parsley, salt and pepper to eggs; mix well.

Heat oil until quite hot. Dip florets in flour and then egg mixture; fry until golden brown all over. Drain. Serve hot.

From Cousin Minnie Rubino, Babylon, N.Y.

CHICK PEAS

2 one-pound cans of chick peas, drained
1½ tablespoons onion, chopped
¼ teaspoon oregano
⅛ teaspoon garlic salt or 1 clove garlic
¼ cup salad oil
⅛ cup red vinegar
Juice of ½ lemon or 2 teaspoons lemon concentrate

Place all ingredients in container with tight lid. Mix well. Cover and refrigerate overnight. Serve as an appetizer.

From Cousin Minnie Rubino, Babylon, N.Y.

CALZONE

1 pound pizza dough
1 pound sausage
1 small ball mozzarella
¼ cup Italian cheese, grated
1 raw egg
1 egg yolk, beaten

Roll out dough in circle. Cook sausage until brown. Cut mozzarella into small cubes. Mix sausage, mozzarella, grated cheese and egg. Spread evenly on dough. Roll up dough. Brush with egg yolk.

Bake in preheated 350-degree oven for 40 minutes. Allow to set for 5 minutes before serving.

From Cousin Molly D. Krosunger, Long Island, N.Y.

CRAB-STUFFED MUSHROOMS

SERVES SIX PEOPLE

20 large mushroom caps
Italian dressing
1½ cups (6½ ounces) canned flaked crabmeat
¾ cup fresh bread crumbs
2 eggs, beaten
½ cup salad dressing
¼ cup onion, minced
1 teaspoon lemon juice

Marinate mushrooms in Italian dressing; drain. Combine crabmeat, ½ cup bread crumbs, eggs, salad dressing, onion and lemon juice.

Fill mushrooms. Top with remaining crumbs. Bake in preheated 350-degree oven 15 minutes.

From Cousin Minnie Rubino, Babylon, N.Y.

MOZZARELLA IN CARROZZA

SERVES SIX PEOPLE

12 slices white bread
6 slices mozzarella or
white American cheese
1 cup milk
¾ cup flour
2 eggs, beaten
½ cup olive or vegetable oil
1 can anchovy fillets, minced
(optional)
1 tablespoon lemon juice
1 clove garlic, minced
(optional)

Trim crusts off bread. Cut cheese to fit bread. Make 6 sandwiches. Dip each in milk, then in flour, finally in eggs. Heat oil in skillet until it starts to bubble. Brown sandwiches on both sides. Remove and drain well.

To oil remaining (if there isn't about ½ cup, add a little more), add anchovies, lemon juice and garlic. Cook 30 seconds, not longer, and pour over sandwiches. Serve hot for lunch, dinner or late evening snack.

Note: These make excellent hors d'oeuvres. Just cut sandwiches into quarters or other desired shapes before dipping in milk.

From my mother, Angelina Valvano, Seaford, N.Y.

MOZZARELLA STICKS

1 small ball mozzarella
2 eggs, well beaten
1 cup flavored bread crumbs
Oil for deep frying
2 tablespoons cheese, grated
(optional)

Cut mozzarella into sticks about 3 inches long and ¼ inch thick. Dip into beaten eggs. Sprinkle grated cheese on bread crumbs. Roll mozzarella in bread crumbs.

Fry in vegetable oil until crisp on all sides. Salt to taste and serve hot.

From Cousin Mary Lou Valvano Fitzgibbons, Rutherford, N.J.

SICILIAN EGGPLANT CAPONATA

SERVES SIX PEOPLE

1 large eggplant
½ cup salad or olive oil
2 onions, chopped
3 ribs celery, chopped
2 cloves garlic, crushed
1 (16-ounce) can Italian-style
tomatoes
10 stuffed olives, chopped
¼ cup capers
¼ cup wine vinegar
3 tablespoons pine nuts
½ teaspoon salt
⅛ teaspoon pepper

Cut unpeeled eggplant into ½-inch cubes. Heat oil in large skillet; add eggplant, onions, celery and garlic. Sauté until tender and eggplant begins to lose its white color.

Stir in tomatoes, olives, capers, vinegar, pine nuts, salt and pepper. Cook uncovered over low heat 20 minutes, stirring occasionally.

Cool and chill. Serve as appetizer or to accompany meats.

From Aunt Josephine Vitale Ricco, Whitestone, N.Y.

STUFFED MUSHROOMS

SERVES SIX PEOPLE

¼ cup olive oil
1 pound large fresh mushrooms
½ cup Parmesan cheese, grated
½ cup fresh Italian
bread crumbs
2 cloves garlic,
chopped very fine
Pinch salt and pepper
Parsley, chopped

Clean mushrooms. Remove stems and chop. Brush mushrooms with oil. Mix cheese, bread crumbs, garlic, salt, pepper, parsley and chopped stems.

Fill mushrooms. Drizzle remaining oil over mushrooms. Pour a little water in bottom of baking dish. Bake in preheated 350-degree oven 20 minutes.

From Cousin Molly D. Krosunger, Long Island, N.Y.

SPINACH BALLS

SERVES SIX PEOPLE

2 (10-ounce) boxes chopped
frozen spinach, thawed and
squeezed dry
2 cups herb stuffing mix
1 large onion, chopped fine
4 eggs, beaten
¾ cup butter, melted
½ cup Parmesan cheese, grated
½ teaspoon garlic salt
¼ teaspoon pepper

Mix all the ingredients; chill overnight. Shape into small balls. Place on greased cookie sheet. Bake in a preheated 350-degree oven 20 minutes.

From Aunt Helen Valvano, Copiague, N.Y.

ZEPPOLI

1 quart milk, lukewarm
2 eggs
2 packages yeast
Dash salt
3 tablespoons butter
About 8 cups flour
Vegetable oil

Beat all ingredients except vegetable oil together and knead until smooth. Let stand at room temperature until it rises and doubles in bulk.

Knead again and let rise again until double. Divide dough into small pieces about size of golf ball. Fry in oil until brown on all sides.

From Aunt Helen Tassani, Corona, N.Y.

SOUPS

STRACCIATELLA ALLA ROMANA

SERVES SIX PEOPLE

2 quarts clear chicken broth
6 eggs
Juice and grated rind
of 2 lemons
1 cup Parmesan cheese, grated
Salt and pepper

Beat eggs with cheese and grated lemon rind. Add salt and pepper to taste. Bring broth to a boil; lower heat until boiling stops.

Slowly add egg mixture to broth, stirring constantly. Bring back to boil; add lemon juice. Cook 5 minutes, stirring occasionally. Serve with extra grated cheese.

From Cousin Minnie Rubino, Babylon, N.Y.

FETTUCCINE ALFREDO

SERVES SIX PEOPLE

1 pound fresh fettuccine pasta
4 tablespoons butter
¾ cup heavy cream
½ cup Parmesan cheese, grated
Freshly ground pepper

Cook fettuccine in plenty of salted water until *al dente* (i.e., not quite tender—literally "to the tooth"). Drain.

Melt butter in large skillet. Add fettuccine and toss until well coated. Combine cream and Parmesan and pour over pasta. Heat until cream is hot and cheese melts, stirring constantly.

From my mother, Angelina Valvano, Seaford, N.Y.

PASTA WITH PRIMAVERA SAUCE

SERVES SIX PEOPLE

1 cup small broccoli florets
1 small zucchini, sliced
1 small red pepper, cut in strips
½ cup frozen peas
¼ cup unsalted butter
1 cup half and half or cream
Pepper
1 pound spaghetti, cooked and drained
Grated cheese

Sauté broccoli, zucchini, red pepper and peas in butter in large skillet until crisp / tender. Add cream and black pepper; cook briefly until slightly reduced.

Serve over spaghetti. Sprinkle with the cheese.

From Cousin Madeline Famularo, Dix Hills, N.Y.

LASAGNE AL FORNO

1 medium onion
3 cloves garlic
3 tablespoons vegetable oil
1½ pounds ground chuck
2 (16-ounce) cans peeled
tomatoes, mashed in blender
1 (8-ounce) can tomato sauce
2 (6-ounce) cans tomato paste
2 envelopes dehydrated
spaghetti sauce mix, prepared
by package directions
2 (12-ounce) cans V-8 juice
4 ounces red wine
2 tablespoons dried parsley
1 tablespoon dried basil
1 sprinkle oregano
Salt and pepper
1 egg
1 pound ricotta cheese
1 (16-ounce) package shredded
mozzarella cheese
¼ cup Parmesan or Romano
cheese, grated
1 pound lasagne

Sauté onions and garlic in oil. Add meat. Brown. Add tomatoes, tomato sauce, tomato paste, wine, spaghetti sauce mix, V-8 juice, herbs (save 1 tablespoon parsley), salt and pepper to taste. Bring to boil. Simmer for 1½ hours.

Mix egg, ricotta, 2 tablespoons Parmesan, 1 tablespoon parsley, dash of salt and pepper in bowl and blend.

Cover bottom of 13-by-9-by-2-inch baking pan with ¼ inch layer of meat sauce. Add layer of raw lasagne, thin layer of ricotta, some Parmesan and mozzarella. Repeat until all lasagne is used, ending with cover of meat sauce.

Cover pan with foil as tightly as possible. Set pan on cookie sheet. Bake 1 hour at 350 degrees. Let stand 1 hour in oven with oven off. Then bake for additional 30 minutes at 325 degrees.

Remove from oven and let sit 30 minutes. Sprinkle on additional parsley and Parmesan. Cut in squares to serve.

From Cousin Anthony Antignano, Corona, N.Y.

SPAGHETTI AGLIATA

½ cup olive oil
½ cup butter
6-8 garlic cloves, minced
1 teaspoon salt
Pepper
½ teaspoon oregano, crumbled
½ cup parsley, finely chopped
1 pound spaghetti, cooked
and drained

Heat oil and butter. Add garlic. Simmer 5 minutes. Add salt, pepper, oregano and parsley. Simmer over low heat 2 minutes. Toss with cooked spaghetti.

From my mother, Angelina Valvano, Seaford, N.Y.

SPAGHETTI CARBONARA

1 pound spaghetti
1 onion, diced
1 tablespoon butter
¼ pound prosciutto, diced
3 chicken bouillon cubes
1 tablespoon parsley
¼ cup water
3 eggs, beaten
¼ pound Fontina cheese, grated
Romano cheese, grated
Black pepper

Cook spaghetti *al dente* according to package directions. Drain.

Half-cook onion in butter in skillet. Add prosciutto, parsley, water and bouillon. Simmer.

Add to spaghetti. Pour eggs onto spaghetti. Quickly lift and mix spaghetti to coat well with egg. Add cheeses and pepper. Mix again.

Note: Heavy cream can be substituted for water.

From Cousin Molly D. Krosunger, Long Island, N.Y.

SPAGHETTI ALLA CARBONARA

¼ pound bacon,
cut into small pieces
1 tablespoon olive oil
or salad oil
1 tablespoon butter
4 eggs, beaten lightly
½ cup Parmesan cheese, grated
Salt and pepper to taste
Parsley, finely minced
(optional)
1 pound spaghetti,
cooked and drained
¼ cup half and half
at room temperature

While spaghetti is cooking, cook bacon in butter and oil. Set aside.

In large skillet or saucepan, mix eggs, cheese, salt and black pepper. Set aside. It is best to have eggs at room temperature so they will not cool off spaghetti so much. As soon as spaghetti is cooked and drained, turn it into skillet with egg-cheese mixture. Add bacon and its cooking fat and stir well; add cream. Dish is ready to serve because the heat of the spaghetti should cook the eggs. However, you can stir spaghetti over very low heat for a minute or two, if you choose. I have turned the spaghetti into a heated serving dish and placed it into a 275-degree oven while I finished getting everything together; heat uncovered for about 15 - 20 minutes.

Stir well and serve with garnish of parsley, if you are using it.

From my mother, Angelina Valvano, Seaford, N.Y.

COLD SPAGHETTI

½ pound mushrooms, sliced
1 tablespoon olive oil
1 eggplant
1 cup olive oil
3 cloves garlic, minced
1 onion, sliced
1 green pepper, sliced in strips
1 (1½-ounce) can anchovy
fillets, chopped fine
12 black olives
1 pound spaghetti
3 tablespoons fresh parsley,
chopped

Sauté mushrooms in 1 tablespoon olive oil.

Peel and slice eggplant, then quarter. Heat ½ cup olive oil in large skillet. Add garlic and sauté until translucent. Add onion and sauté until light brown. Add eggplant and sauté until golden. Add peppers and sauté.

Remove pan from heat. Add anchovies, olives and sautéed mushrooms.

In large pot of boiling water, cook spaghetti until *al dente*. Drain and toss immediately with remaining ½ cup olive oil. Toss with eggplant mixture. Let cool completely. Just before serving, add parsley and mix well.

From Cousin James Vitale, Island Park, N.Y.

SPINACH-NOODLE CASSEROLE

6 ounces noodles
1 (10-ounce) package frozen
chopped spinach
1 envelope Hollandaise
sauce mix
½ teaspoon dry mustard
¾ cup water
1 cup sour cream
¼ cup Parmesan cheese, grated
½ teaspoon salt
¼ cup seasoned bread crumbs
2 tablespoons Parmesan
cheese, grated
1 tablespoon butter, melted

Cook noodles as directed on package. Cook spinach. Drain each. Set aside.

In a saucepan, combine Hollandaise sauce mix and mustard; stir in water. Cook and stir until bubbly. Stir in sour cream. Combine with noodles, spinach, ¼ cup Parmesan and salt.

Turn into ungreased 1½-quart casserole. Bake, covered, in preheated 350-degree oven 20 minutes.

Combine bread crumbs, 2 tablespoons Parmesan and butter. Sprinkle on top. Bake 10 minutes more.

From Cousin Madeline Famularo, Dix Hills, N.Y.

WHITE CLAM SAUCE

2 (7½-ounce) cans
minced clams
¼ cup olive oil
¼ cup butter
2 cloves garlic, minced
2 tablespoons fresh parsley,
chopped
1½ teaspoons salt

Drain clams; reserve ¾ cup liquid. Set aside.

Slowly heat oil and butter in skillet. Add garlic; sauté until golden. Remove from heat.

Stir in clam liquid, parsley and salt. Bring to boil; reduce heat; simmer 3 minutes. Return clams to sauce; heat gently. Serve over ½ pound pasta.

From Cousin Minnie Rubino, Babylon, N.Y.

CHICKEN & CRAB DELIGHT

SERVES FOUR PEOPLE

4 chicken cutlets
(boneless breasts)
White wine
1 lemon
7 teaspoons butter
Garlic, parsley, onion, chopped

Place breasts side by side in baking dish. (Do not overlap.) Pour in enough wine to cover ¾ of meat. Add lemon juice from squeezed lemon, butter, garlic, parsley and onion.

Bake in preheated 350-degree oven until breasts are barely done. Baste continuously to keep moist. When breasts are cooking, prepare crabmeat topping.

CRABMEAT TOPPING

1 package slivered almonds
8 ounces cream cheese, softened
1 package frozen snow crab
2 tablespoons onion, finely chopped
1 teaspoon horseradish
Salt and pepper to taste

Mix together cheese, crab, onion, horseradish, salt, pepper and ½ package almonds. Place mixture in ovenproof bowl or dish. Bake at 350 degrees for 10 minutes.

Spoon mixture onto chicken cutlets. Top with remaining slivered almonds and bake 5-10 minutes more.

From brother Bobby Valvano and his wife Darlene, Brooklyn, N.Y.

CHICKEN IN BEER

1-2 chickens, cut up
1-2 (12-ounce) cans beer
1 stick butter
1 medium onion, chopped

In heavy pan or Dutch oven, melt butter. Add onions and chicken. Cook on high until chicken is golden brown. Lower heat and add beer. Simmer chicken, covered, until tender, about 45 minutes to 1 hour.

Serve over boiled rice.

From Aunt Helen Tassani, Corona, N.Y.

CHICKEN ROLLATINI

SERVES SIX PEOPLE

6 boneless chicken breasts
6 slices prosciutto
6 slices mozzarella cheese
6 slices Genoa salami
6 quarters hard-boiled eggs
Fresh garlic, minced
Olive oil
Salt and pepper
Grated cheese
Sweet basil
Parsley
1 small can tomato sauce
2 cups sauterne

Put chicken between 2 pieces of waxed paper and pound till thin. Sprinkle each chicken breast with olive oil, salt, pepper and grated cheese. Top each breast with piece of prosciutto, mozzarella, salami and boiled egg. Sprinkle with garlic, basil and parsley.

Roll up each piece and tie. Put in pan; cover with tomato sauce and sauterne. Bake in preheated 350-degree oven for 45-60 minutes.

From Aunt Rosemary Mesiti, Flushing, N.Y.

CHICKEN IN GARLIC SAUCE

SERVES SIX PEOPLE

3 chickens, 2½-3 pounds
each, cut up
1 large can Italian tomatoes
1 garlic head, mashed fine
Italian parsley, chopped
½ cup olive oil
Juice of 4 lemons
Salt, pepper, oregano

Mix all ingredients and pour over chicken. Bake in 350-degree oven for 1 hour and 10 minutes.

From Aunt Annette Celano, Syosset, N.Y.

ESCAROLE & SPARE RIBS

SERVES SIX PEOPLE

2 pounds escarole
2 pounds pork ribs
3 cloves garlic, minced
3 tablespoons olive oil
1 tablespoon salt
Romano cheese

In large Dutch oven or large frying pan, heat oil. Add spare ribs. Brown well on both sides. Add garlic and sauté for 1 minute. Cover and simmer 1 hour or until meat is very well done.

Cook escarole in 2 quarts salted, boiling water until tender. Reserve the water. (Jim likes the escarole very tender, not crisp.) Add escarole plus 2 cups escarole water to cooked ribs. Simmer 5 minutes.

Flavor improves if it stands an hour or so before serving. Sprinkle with Romano cheese and serve with Italian bread.

From my mother, Angelina Valvano, Seaford, N.Y.

ITALIAN QUICHE WITH SAUSAGE

1 frozen pie shell
½ pound sweet hot pork sausages
1 large tomato, skinned and chopped
½ teaspoon salt
¼ teaspoon pepper
½ teaspoon each oregano, basil, parsley
1½ cups ricotta cheese
4 eggs, lightly beaten

Bake pie shell in preheated 450-degree oven for 15 minutes. Remove from oven. Turn oven down to 375 degrees.

Cook sausages in skillet until brown. Pour off excess fat and add tomato, salt, pepper and herbs. Cook 2 - 3 minutes.

Whip ricotta. Add eggs. Beat until smooth. Add to sausage. Pour into pie shell. Bake 30 minutes at 375 degrees.

From Cousin Molly D. Krosunger, Long Island, N.Y.

ITALIAN SAUSAGE WITH POTATOES

1 pound Italian sausage, sweet or hot
4 medium potatoes, boiled, peeled and diced
½ teaspoon salt
½ teaspoon pepper
(omit if using hot sausage)

Prick sausage with needle, place in large frying pan with 1 tablespoon water and brown thoroughly. Add potatoes and brown in sausage fat. Add salt and pepper, cut sausage into bite-size pieces and serve.

From Cousin Mary Lou Valvano Fitzgibbons, Rutherford, N.J.

MUSSELS (FRA DIAVOLA) MARINARA

SERVES FOUR PEOPLE

3 pounds fresh mussels
3 (16-ounce) cans Italian
tomatoes, drained and crushed
2 teaspoons olive oil
1 - 2 teaspoons crushed
hot pepper
1 dash hot sauce
1 dash oregano
1 clove garlic
½ cup Marsala
Salt and pepper
1 pound linguine or spaghetti

In large saucepan, brown garlic in olive oil over medium heat. Do not burn. Add oregano and stir. Add tomatoes, but DO NOT ADD liquid. Bring to boil. Once pot boils, add rest of ingredients, EXCEPT mussels. Reduce to simmer and cook for 2½ hours.

While sauce is cooking, put fresh mussels in colander with cold water running through them for about 15 minutes. Then scrub and clean with vegetable brush.

When sauce is done, place scrubbed mussels gently in pot and simmer until they are opened and tender (about 20 minutes).

Cook pasta. Serve mussels on top with remaining sauce. Mangia!!

From Cousin Paula Morelli, Bohemia, N.Y.

PASTIERRA

1½ cups (9 ounces) egg pastene
6 cups boiling water
1 teaspoon salt
3 links (6 ounces) semi-dried sausage
4 eggs
2 tablespoons Parmesan cheese, grated
¼ teaspoon pepper

Grease 9-inch pie plate. Cook pastene in boiling water with salt for 5 minutes. Drain well. Halve sausage lengthwise; slice ¼ inch thick.

Beat eggs in large bowl. Mix in pastene, sausage, Parmesan, pepper and salt to taste. Pour into pie plate.

Bake in preheated 350-degree oven for 1 hour. Remove and let stand 5 minutes before cutting.

From Cousin James Vitale, Island Park, N.Y.

SALTIMBOCCA

1 pound thin veal cutlets, pounded
1½ slices thin prosciutto, cut into 2-inch strips
Sage leaves, crumbled
¼ cup Romano cheese, grated
Salt and pepper
½ cup butter

Cut veal into 2-inch squares. On each square, place strip of prosciutto, crumbled sage leaf and some cheese. Roll square up carefully. Fasten with toothpick lengthwise. Sprinkle with salt and pepper.

Heat butter in large skillet. Cook veal rolls over moderate heat until golden brown on all sides. When done, remove toothpicks. Serve with drippings left in pan.

From Aunt Annette Celano, Syosset, N.Y.
(Mrs. Celano is my godmother.)

SAUTÉED GARLIC CRABS

SERVES SIX PEOPLE

1 dozen crabs (blue claw)
½ pound butter
6 garlic cloves, minced
1/3 cup olive oil
1/3 cup chablis
1 teaspoon garlic powder
Parsley flakes
Salt and pepper

Place crabs in pot of boiling water. When they turn red (approximately 10 minutes), remove and allow to cool. Remove back of crab and rinse thoroughly. Make sure to remove "dead man" of crab also. Put aside.

In saucepan, sauté and simmer all other ingredients for 1½ hours. After sauce is done, place crabs in baking pan, pouring sauce on top. Garnish top with parsley flakes. Cover tightly with aluminum foil, making sure that no air gets in. Bake crabs and sauce at 350 degrees for 15 more minutes. Uncover and enjoy!!

From Cousin Paula Morelli, Bohemia, N.Y.

SPARE RIBS & SAUSAGES

SERVES SIX PEOPLE

1 pound spare ribs
6 sausages
3 tablespoons oil
Red pepper
½ teaspoon salt
1 cup dry red wine
4 cups tomatoes

Cook sausages by putting water in pan and cooking until browned and water is evaporated.

Cut up spare ribs and brown in oil for 5 or 10 minutes. Add pepper to taste, salt, wine and tomatoes; bring to boil. Add sausages. Lower heat and simmer for 1 hour.

From Aunt Annette Celano, Syosset, N.Y.

SKILLET SHRIMP PRONTO

SERVES FOUR PEOPLE

1½ pounds unpeeled raw shrimp
4 vine-ripe tomatoes, peeled and diced
1 onion, peeled and minced
1 clove garlic, minced (optional)
2 teaspoons olive oil
½ cup dry white wine
1 tablespoon fresh parsley, minced
2 teaspoons fresh oregano, minced
Salt and pepper to taste
4 tablespoons Romano cheese, grated

Remove shells and black veins from shrimp. Rinse; dry; set aside.

Combine onion, garlic, olive oil and 1 tablespoon wine in nonstick skillet. Cook and stir until wine evaporates and onion begins to brown. Stir in tomatoes, parsley, oregano and remaining wine; heat to simmering. Simmer uncovered for 5 minutes.

Arrange shrimp on top of tomato mixture; continue to simmer until shrimp is pink, 2 - 5 minutes more, depending on size. Season to taste. Sprinkle with cheese.

From brother Nick Valvano, New York, N.Y.

STUFFED PORK CHOPS

SERVES FOUR PEOPLE

4 (1-inch thick) pork chops
3 links Italian sausage
2 tablespoons butter
½ box frozen chopped spinach, cooked and drained
3 tablespoons Parmesan cheese
1 egg
½ cup chicken broth

Remove casing from sausages and sauté in butter. Add spinach, egg and cheese. Mix thoroughly and cook slowly for 3 minutes.

Make a pocket in each pork chop, stuff with some of mixture and brown each side in frying pan. Place browned chop in baking pan. Add chicken broth. Bake in 350-degree oven for 45 minutes, or until broth evaporates.

From Aunt Josephine Vitale Ricco, Whitestone, N.Y.

VEAL CUTLETS PARMIGIANA

1 pound veal cutlets
Bread crumbs
2 eggs
2 tablespoons Parmesan or
Romano cheese, grated
5 tablespoons olive oil
Salt and pepper
¾ pound mozzarella, sliced
Homemade Tomato Sauce

Add salt and pepper to eggs. Beat thoroughly. Mix bread crumbs and cheese. Dip cutlets in eggs and roll in bread crumbs. Sauté breaded cutlets in hot oil until nicely browned on each side.

Place cutlets in baking dish; cover with little tomato sauce. Top each cutlet with thin slices of mozzarella.

Bake in slow oven 15 minutes or until mozzarella turns golden brown and chops are cooked through. Serve hot with more tomato sauce.

HOMEMADE TOMATO SAUCE

1 small onion or 2 cloves of
garlic, chopped
4 tablespoons butter
1 (16-ounce) can plum
tomatoes (Italian style)
½ can tomato paste (Italian
style), dissolved in small
amount of water
1 teaspoon sugar
1 teaspoon basil leaf, chopped
Salt and pepper to taste

Sauté onion or garlic in butter. Add tomatoes, tomato paste, sugar, basil, salt and pepper. Simmer for 30 minutes.

From my mother, Angelina Valvano, Seaford, N.Y.

VEAL FRANCESE

SERVES SIX PEOPLE

2 pounds veal cutlets
cut very thin
Salt and pepper
3 eggs, beaten lightly
Flour for dredging
4 tablespoons olive oil
6 tablespoons butter
Juice of 1 lemon
Thin lemon slices
Parsley for garnish

Sprinkle veal slices with salt and pepper. Dip into beaten egg and dredge in flour. Shake off excess flour.

In large skillet, heat 4 tablespoons each olive oil and butter and sauté veal slices on both sides. As veal is cooked, set aside on warm platter or place in warming oven.

When all veal is cooked, add 2 additional tablespoons butter to skillet with lemon juice. Cook for 30 seconds; pour sauce over veal. Garnish with lemon slices and chopped parsley.

From my mother, Angelina Valvano, Seaford, N.Y.

VEAL MARSALA

1 pound very thin veal cutlets
¼ cup flour
Salt
Pepper
3 tablespoons butter or margarine
¼ cup Marsala wine
Parsley

Cut cutlets in small pieces. Sprinkle with salt and pepper; coat lightly with flour.

Sauté cutlets in butter or margarine 2 minutes on each side or until golden. Remove to heated platter.

To remaining butter in skillet, add Marsala wine. Simmer 1 minute, stirring to loosen browned bits of veal. If desired, return veal to sauce and simmer gently, 2 - 5 minutes.

Pour sauce over veal on platter; garnish with parsley.

From Cousin Minnie Rubino, Babylon, N.Y.

VEGETABLES

ARTICHOKE BOTTOMS
STUFFED WITH CHOPPED MUSHROOMS

SERVES FOUR PEOPLE

1 pound (4 cups) medium-sized
mushrooms, finely chopped
½ cup shallots, finely chopped
¼ cup olive oil
2 tablespoons parsley, chopped
1½ teaspoons fresh thyme,
chopped, or ½ teaspoon leaf
thyme, crumbled
¼ teaspoon salt
⅛ teaspoon pepper
2 tablespoons heavy cream
1 (14-ounce) can artichoke
bottoms

Sauté mushrooms and shallots in oil in large skillet over high heat. Stir and cook for 5 minutes. Stir in 1 tablespoon parsley and thyme, salt, pepper and cream.

Spoon into artichoke bottoms. Keep warm in slow oven. Garnish with remaining parsley.

From Cousin James Vitale, Island Park, N.Y.

ARTICHOKE PIE

SERVES FOUR PEOPLE

1 package frozen artichoke
hearts, thawed and drained
4 eggs, well beaten
½ cup pepperoni, diced
1 cup mozzarella cheese, diced
¼ cup Romano cheese, grated
1 unbaked 9-inch pie shell

Pat artichoke hearts dry. Cut in half. Mix with eggs, pepperoni, mozzarella, salt, pepper and cheeses. Pour into pie crust. Bake at 350 degrees for 45 minutes.

From Cousin Molly D. Krosunger, Long Island, N.Y.

AUNT JOSIE'S ARTICHOKES

4 artichokes
2 cups Italian bread (stale)
½ cup Romano cheese, grated
1 clove garlic, minced
Salt and pepper to taste
2 tablespoons parsley,
finely chopped
6 tablespoons olive oil

Remove tough outer leaves from artichokes. Cut off stem and ½ inch of artichoke leaves. Wash and drain. Tap the artichokes on table to spread leaves open.

Soak bread. Remove crust and squeeze water out completely. About 2 cups of bread needed. Add cheese, garlic, salt and pepper, parsley and 2 tablespoons of olive oil. Mix thoroughly.

Divide mixture into 4 parts. Distribute 1 portion between leaves of each artichoke, then close.

Place artichoke upright in saucepan so that each fits snugly. Pour 1 tablespoon olive oil over each artichoke. Add 1 cup of water. Cover tightly.

Cook slowly for ½ hour or until done. Test by pulling outer leaf. If leaf is removed easily, artichoke is done.

From Aunt Josephine Vitale Ricco, Whitestone, N.Y.

GOLDEN FRIED ZUCCHINI

SERVES FOUR PEOPLE

8 small zucchini, sliced
2 cups olive oil
1 cup flour
Salt and pepper

Wash zucchini. Do not peel. Cut into narrow lengthwise strips. Sprinkle with salt and let stand for 1 hour in colander.

Roll in flour and fry in hot oil until golden crisp. Sprinkle with salt and pepper and serve immediately.

From Aunt Helen Tassani, Corona, N.Y.

ITALIAN POTATO PUFF

SERVES SIX PEOPLE

2 cups potatoes, peeled, boiled and mashed
½ cup onion, chopped
2 tablespoons parsley, chopped
1 cup ricotta cheese
½ cup Parmesan cheese, grated
3 eggs
1 teaspoon salt
½ teaspoon garlic, minced very finely
⅛ teaspoon black pepper
2 tablespoons butter, melted
8 ounces mozzarella cheese, sliced

Combine potatoes, onions, parsley, ricotta, Parmesan cheese, eggs, salt, garlic, pepper and butter. Mix well.

Spread half the mixture into a buttered, 8-inch-square baking dish. Cover with half the sliced mozzarella. Spread remaining potato mixture on top and add another layer of mozzarella. Sprinkle with Parmesan cheese. Cover with aluminum foil.

Bake in preheated 350-degree oven 30 minutes. Remove foil and continue baking 15 minutes or until cheese is bubbling.

From Aunt Helen Valvano, Copiague, N.Y.

NEOPOLITAN PEAS & EGGS

1 small onion, chopped
1 tablespoon vegetable oil
2 (8-ounce) cans tomato sauce
½ cup water
1 (20-ounce) bag frozen peas
¼ teaspoon pepper
5 eggs

Sauté onion in oil in large skillet until tender. Add tomato sauce and water. Bring to boil. Add peas and pepper. Cook over high heat until peas have separated and thawed. Lower heat.

Break eggs onto pea mixture, making certain eggs are far enough apart to cook separately. Cover tightly. Simmer 5-10 minutes or until eggs are cooked to desired doneness.

This egg and vegetable combination would make a good brunch dish.

From Cousin James Vitale, Island Park, N.Y.

PEAS & EGGS

SERVES FOUR PEOPLE

4 eggs
1 small can tomato sauce
1 medium can peas, drained
½ onion, chopped
1 tablespoon vegetable oil
Salt and pepper

Sauté onion in oil in skillet until soft. Add tomato sauce; simmer for 5 minutes. Add peas, salt and pepper. Simmer about 10 minutes. Drop eggs in sunny-side up. Cover skillet until eggs are poached. Easy and good.

From Aunt Johanna Tamberino, Corona, N.Y.

POTATO CROQUETTES

SERVES FIVE PEOPLE

5 potatoes
2 eggs
1 cup bread crumbs
½ cup Italian cheese, grated
½ teaspoon parsley
1 teaspoon salt
½ teaspoon pepper
Flour
Extra bread crumbs
Oil

Boil potatoes until just done enough to mash. Mash. Add eggs, 1 cup bread crumbs, cheese, parsley, salt and pepper.

Shape into ½-inch patties. Roll in flour and bread crumbs. Brown in oil until golden brown. Drain.

From Cousin Adele Balemian, Melville, Long Island, N.Y.

SCALLOPED EGGPLANT

1 eggplant (1½ pounds)
2 tablespoons butter
1 small onion, chopped fine
1 tablespoon parsley,
finely chopped
Salt
Freshly ground pepper
Buttered bread crumbs
Parmesan cheese, grated

Peel eggplant; cut into ½-inch cubes. Put eggplant in a pot with 1 inch boiling water; cover and cook gently until tender, about 5 - 10 minutes. Drain.

Melt butter in skillet, add onion and cook over low heat until soft but not brown. Stir in eggplant and parsley; season with salt and pepper; combine gently.

Spoon into buttered baking dish, cover with lots of bread crumbs and grated cheese. Bake in preheated 375-degree oven until eggplant is heated through and the crumbs are brown.

From Aunt Helen Valvano, Copiague, N.Y.

STRING BEAN PIE

2 pounds string beans
4 large boiled potatoes in jackets
2 bunches scallions
5 eggs
Italian cheese to taste, grated
Salt and pepper
2 tablespoons butter
½ cup bread crumbs
4 tablespoons vegetable oil

Cook string beans until done. Put through blender. Peel and mash boiled potatoes, adding butter. Sauté scallions and beans in 2 tablespoons oil until scallions are tender. Add mashed potatoes, cheese and eggs.

Mix bread crumbs and 2 tablespoons oil, salt and pepper to taste. Line bottom of cookie sheet with bread crumb mixture. Put bean-potato mixture over bread crumbs. Bake in preheated 325-degree oven for 30 minutes. Cut into squares.

From Aunt Johanna Tamberino, Corona, N.Y.

THREE-BEAN SALAD

1 can cannellini beans, drained
1 can kidney beans, drained
1 can chickpeas, drained
3 scallions, chopped
½ - 1 cup olive oil
Juice of 3 lemons
3 - 4 stalks celery, diced
½ - 1 cup parsley, chopped
Salt and pepper to taste

Place beans in serving bowl. Add rest of ingredients.

Mix well. Serve slightly chilled.

From Cousin Molly D. Krosunger, Long Island, N.Y.

STUFFED ARTICHOKES

6 fresh artichokes
2 cups bread crumbs
1 cup Parmesan or Romano cheese, grated
½ cup parsley, chopped
3 cloves garlic, minced
1 tablespoon oregano
½ teaspoon pepper
6 cloves garlic, cut in half
Water
Salt to taste
¼ cup olive oil (or to taste)

With one push of a sharp, heavy knife, cut off the upper part of each artichoke at a point 1 to 1½ inches from the top. With a pair of scissors, snip off the top of the outside petals remaining below that point. Cut the stem off, making a flat base. Using a sharp spoon, dig out the center petals and the "choke."

Mix next 6 ingredients in large bowl. Take each artichoke and, standing it in the bowl of seasoned crumbs, spread the petals apart with your fingers. Force in as much crumb mixture as it will hold.

Stand the artichokes in a large pot; sprinkle garlic pieces around the bottom; add water to a depth of 1 inch; salt to taste; drizzle olive oil over the tops; and simmer, covered, until tender, about 30 minutes. Serve hot or lukewarm, passing some of the cooking liquid for dipping at the table.

From Aunt Helen Valvano, Copiague, N.Y.

BREADS & BEVERAGES

CARROT BREAD

SERVES SIX PEOPLE

2 cups flour
1½ cups sugar
2 teaspoons cinnamon
½ teaspoon salt
2 teaspoons baking soda
1 cup vegetable oil
3 eggs
½ cup raisins, diced
¼ cup coconut
½ cup walnuts
2 cups carrots, grated

Combine all ingredients and mix thoroughly. Pour into 2 greased bread pans and let stand 20 minutes. Bake in preheated 350-degree oven 1 hour.

From Cousin Adele Balemian, Melville, Long Island, N.Y.

ITALIAN SAUSAGE BREAD

SERVES SIX PEOPLE

1 pound pizza dough
2 pounds Italian sausage
½ pound mozzarella, grated
¼ cup Romano cheese, grated
1 raw egg
1 egg yolk

Roll out dough in circle. Cook sausage without casing. Drain on paper towel.

Mix sausage, mozzarella, Romano and egg. Spread evenly on pizza dough. Roll up and place on cookie sheet with all seams turned down. Brush top with egg yolk. Bake in 350-degree oven 35 minutes.

From my mother, Angelina Valvano, Seaford, N.Y.

EGGNOG PUNCH

1 quart eggnog
1 pint heavy cream
1 pint vanilla ice cream
½ pint light rum
Sprinkle of nutmeg

Pour eggnog, cream and ice cream into blender bowl and whip on high. Add rum and whip again.

From Cousin Madeline Famularo, Dix Hills, N.Y.

DESSERTS

APPLE CRISP

SERVES SIX PEOPLE

2 cups tart apples,
peeled and sliced
½ teaspoon cinnamon
½ teaspoon nutmeg
Juice of ½ lemon
¼ cup water
½ cup butter
½ cup flour
1 cup brown sugar

Place sliced apples in a greased rectangular baking dish; sprinkle with cinnamon, nutmeg, lemon juice and water.

Blend butter, flour and brown sugar until crumbly. Spread over apples.

Bake in preheated 350-degree oven for 30 minutes. Serve hot with heavy cream.

From Cousin Minnie Rubino, Babylon, N.Y.

BISCUIT TORTONI

SERVES SIX PEOPLE

8 stale macaroons,
broken in pieces
¾ cup rich milk
¼ cup confectioner's sugar
1 cup heavy cream
1 teaspoon vanilla
Toasted almonds
Maraschino cherries
Few grains salt

Place macaroons in blender, about 4 at a time. Blend until finely chopped. Combine crushed macaroons, milk, sugar and salt; let sit one hour. Whip cream until stiff; fold into macaroon mixture. Add vanilla.

Place mixture in paper muffin cups in muffin tin; freeze. When set, decorate with cherries and almonds.

From Cousin Minnie Rubino, Babylon, N.Y.

CREAM CHEESE POUND CAKE

SERVES SIX PEOPLE

½ pound butter, softened
¼ pound cream cheese, softened
2 cups sugar
3 cups flour
5 eggs
1 cup milk
2 teaspoons vanilla

Blend butter and cream cheese with sugar. Add eggs 1 at a time. Add flour and milk, alternately. Add vanilla.

Pour into greased tube pan and bake in preheated 350-degree oven for 1 hour. Serve with whipped cream, ice cream or fruit.

From Aunt Rosemary Mesiti, Flushing, N.Y.

ITALIAN CHEESE CAKE

SERVES SIX PEOPLE

2 tablespoons butter
About 10 zwieback or graham crackers
1 cup sugar
2 pounds ricotta, drained very well
¼ cup flour
½ cup heavy cream
2 tablespoons lemon juice
1 teaspoon lemon rind, grated
1 teaspoon vanilla
4 eggs, well beaten

Butter bottom and sides of 9-inch springform pan. Roll crackers to fine crumbs. Mix with a little of sugar. Coat bottom and sides of pan. Save 2 tablespoons sugar to sprinkle on top of cake.

Combine rest of sugar and remaining ingredients. Beat well. Pour into pan. Sprinkle on reserved sugar. Bake in preheated 325-degree oven for 1 hour or until cake is almost firm in middle.

From Cousin Molly D. Krosunger, Long Island, N.Y.

LA PLACITA SOPAIPILLA

4 cups soft flour
¾ teaspoon salt
2 teaspoons baking powder
1 tablespoon shortening
1 cup warm water

Mix dry ingredients. Add shortening and mix until it is thoroughly dissolved. Slowly add warm water and knead dough until smooth. Dough should be about the consistency of pie dough, or possibly a little stiffer.

Cover the dough with a damp cloth and let rise for about one hour. Roll dough out very thin, about 1/32 of an inch; cut into rectangular strips about ¾ inches wide. Cook in deep fat, shortening or oil at about 400 degrees. Cook as you would with doughnuts, immersing and turning the pastry until it is golden brown. Serve hot with butter and honey.

Note:
The sopaipillas puff up as they are cooked. If they do not puff sufficiently, it is either because the oil or shortening is not hot enough, or because the dough was not rolled thin enough.

From Aunt Helen Valvano, Copiague, N.Y.

PABASINOS

6 cups flour
2 cups vegetable shortening
1½ cups sugar
½ teaspoon salt
2 tablespoons water
1 cup walnuts, chopped
1 cup white raisins
2 tablespoons orange rind, chopped fine

Mix flour, salt, shortening, sugar and water. Remove from bowl and place on floured surface. Press flat with hand. Cover surface with walnuts, raisins and orange rind, then knead into ball. This will allow raisins, rind and nuts to mix well through dough.

Cut into sections. Roll each ¾ inch thick and 2½ inches long.

Bake in preheated 350-degree oven 25-30 minutes or until light brown. Cool and ice with frosting of your choice.

From Aunt Frances Valvano, via Vita Lohr, Long Island, N.Y.

PASTIERO DI GRANO (Easter Wheat Pie)

1- 1½ cups cooked wheat
(available at import stores)
½ cup scalded cream or half and half
¼ teaspoon salt
¼ teaspoon sugar
1½ pounds ricotta
1 cup sugar
6 egg yolks, beaten
1 tablespoon orange water
¼ cup citron, diced
¼ cup orange peel, diced
4 egg whites, beaten stiff
1 teaspoon vanilla
Pasta Frolla
Confectioner's sugar

Add wheat, ¼ teaspoon sugar and salt to scalded cream. Boil 5 minutes. Remove from heat. Add citron and orange peel. Set aside.

Beat ricotta and 1 cup sugar. Add egg yolks, vanilla, orange water. Blend well. Stir in wheat mixture. Fold in beaten egg whites. Pour into Pasta Frolla (pie shell).

Arrange strips of pastry to make lattice topping over filling. Turn bottom overhang up over strips at edge and flute.

Bake in preheated 350-degree oven for 1 hour or until firm in center. Let cool in oven with door open. Sprinkle when cooled with confectioner's sugar.

PASTA FROLLA
(Flaky Sweet Pie Crust)

2 cups flour, sifted
½ cup sugar
Pinch of salt
¼ cup butter
3 egg yolks
1 tablespoon milk

Sift flour and sugar. Cut in butter with pastry blender or fingertips. Stir in egg yolks, 1 at a time, mixing with wooden spoon.

Work dough with hands until manageable. Add milk to hold together. Turn onto lightly floured wooden board. Knead until smooth.

Form into ball and chill for 30 minutes. Divide into 2 balls.

Roll 1 ball out on lightly floured board to make circle that is ⅛ inch thick and is large enough to fit 10-inch pie plate. Line buttered pie plate with 1 crust, leaving ½ - inch overhang.

Roll and cut other half into ¾-inch strips for latticework topping.

From Cousin Molly D. Krosunger, Long Island, N.Y.

SICILIAN CREAM CAKE

1 box yellow cake mix
1¼ pounds ricotta
1 cup fine sugar
1 teaspoon vanilla
2 teaspoons liqueur
2 tablespoons candied fruit,
cut in small pieces
1 tablespoon chocolate bits
Powdered sugar
Whipping cream

Bake cake and cool. Place ricotta, sugar, vanilla, liqueur, fruit and chocolate bits in bowl and mix well with wooden spoon until smooth and fluffy. This will take about 10 minutes.

Cut cake in 1-inch slices and line bottom and sides of 9-by-13-inch pan with cake. Pour part of ricotta cream over cake. Repeat with cake, then cream mixture. Store in refrigerator overnight.

Before serving, turn out on serving dish and sprinkle with powdered sugar or whipped cream.

From Aunt Annette Celano, Syosset, N.Y.

STRUFFOLI

2½ cups flour
4 eggs
1 egg yolk
½ cup leaf lard or vegetable shortening
1½ teaspoons sugar
⅛ teaspoon salt
½ teaspoon lemon peel, grated
Oil for frying
2 cups (approximately) honey
1 teaspoon orange peel, grated

Place flour on board and make well in center. Into it place eggs, egg yolk, sugar, shortening, salt and lemon peel. Mix well with hands, working dough quickly. Shape into very thin balls (size is up to you). Heat oil to high temperature for deep frying (about 375 degrees).

Carefully lower balls, a few at a time, into oil and cook. Drain on paper towels.

Meanwhile, in saucepan, heat honey and add orange peel. Drop balls into this mixture to coat, then drain them and place on a serving dish.

Allow struffoli to cool, then dip hands into cold water and arrange balls in desired shape, generally a pyramid. Pyramid may be decorated with different colored candies, cherries, chopped nuts, silver dragees or confetti for a festive look.

Note:
This dish is a traditional Christmas custom for Italian families.

From my mother, Angelina Valvano, Seaford, N.Y.

ZUPPA INGLESE

36 ladyfingers
¼ cup rum
1 package vanilla pudding mix
2 cups milk
2 packages chocolate
pudding mix
4 cups milk
1 cup heavy cream, whipped
1/3 cup (about) candied fruit
¼ cup (about) toasted almonds

Spread ladyfingers on waxed paper. Sprinkle rum onto open surfaces.

Meanwhile, make vanilla and chocolate puddings in separate saucepans, according to package directions. Allow to cool. (Place waxed paper directly on surface of cooling pudding, to prevent crust from forming.)

To assemble, have ready a pretty 8-cup dessert bowl. Line bowl sides and bottoms with ladyfingers. Spoon in half of chocolate. Top with half of vanilla pudding. Layer with half of remaining chocholate, rest of vanilla, ending with chocolate. This should reach top of the bowl.

Finish by topping pudding with mounds of whipped cream. Sprinkle on candied fruit and almonds. Refrigerate until ready to serve.

From my mother, Angelina Valvano, Seaford, N.Y.

"1 LOBSTER TAIL, 1 BURGER"

My first date with my wife Pam was February 10, 1962. It was the Junior Prom at Seaford High School, and our romance nearly ended right there. All because of a lobster tail.

Let me tell you about it.

I'd known Pam since the eighth grade when we were in the same homeroom. But we'd never dated. She was busy with older men, and I was busy with sports.

We were always friends, though, and since her regular boyfriend was away at college, I asked her to the prom.

Afterwards we went to dinner at Karl Hoppl's restaurant on Long Island. I should have known right then and there she was going to be trouble. She ordered lobster tail. Back then I didn't even know lobsters had tails, much less that you ate them.

After she ordered, I looked at the menu and then I excused myself. I went into the men's room and took out my wallet to see if I had enough money to pay for this lobster tail. I figured out ONE of us could have lobster tail but that the other one was going to have to have tunafish or a burger. Guess who had the burger?

Well, anyway, I got her back for ordering the most expensive thing on Karl Hoppl's menu—only it *was* an accident and maybe even a little poetic justice.

Shortly afterwards, you see, I took Pam to the movies. You know how women will always say "no" when you ask them if they want their own soda and popcorn—then end up eating half of yours. (Pam used to say, "It's just nicer to eat yours.")

So, here I am in a dark theater, bent over, trying to squeeze my way between people's knees and the backs of the seats in front. And I stumble, and spill Coke all over her lap. Both of us knew it was an accident—and it didn't really put a damper (pun intended) on our relationship from there on out. But Pam says now, "I should have known at that point what kind of *character* you are!"

We dated all four years while I was at Rutgers University. (During that time she went to business school and later worked for *Look* magazine in Manhattan.) Then we got engaged the summer before my senior year in college and were married on August 6, 1967.

My wife's maiden name was Pamela Sue Levine. She, too, was born in the Big Apple, and moved to Seaford, Long Island, when she was nine.

She comes from a very small family. Her late father, Arnold, was the son of a Russian Jew who had immigrated here; and her mother, Wilma, was a first-generation American whose parents came here from Glasgow, Scotland. (Ironically, my family lives on Glasgow Road in Cary today!)

Although her parents did not keep kosher, they did have the Friday-night dinners and the lighting of the candles and went to temple. And they always had Passover Seders and things like that. In fact, they wrote out parts of the ceremony of the Seder in phonetics so Rocco and Angelina's boy Jim could join in the celebration of the Jewish people's "Festival of Freedom," which commemorates the flight of the Children of Israel from Egypt.

Because her Mom had been raised Protestant, Pam's family celebrated Christmas, too. So what we got, when we tied the knot, was two whole sets of holidays!

At that time ours was considered a "mixed marriage"—which was more unusual then than now. And I was not only the first in my family to marry a non-Catholic; I was one of the first to marry a non-Italian!

But food—and especially the holiday dinners we shared at her house and my house—proved a great icebreaker. As Pam says, "Your aunts and uncles accepted me and loved me and made me feel like part of the family—even when we were just dating."

The only difference, then and now, is that Pam doesn't have an Italian appetite. In fact, I think it was at the first Thanksgiving dinner with my family that she came to me after the antipasto and pasta parts and said, well, it had been a great spread and she'd enjoyed the dinner a lot. I said, "Babe, we're just beginning!" And we went on to the meat part and the vegetables and the salads and the desserts—for hours. I explained to her afterwards that if you have a small appetite like hers, you just have a little "taste" of everything.

Eating with Pam and her parents and brother, Ron, really broadened my culinary horizons. My mother would try anything once—Italian, American, whatever—but my father was strictly a meat-and-potatoes man, then and now. So Mom didn't get a chance to experiment much.

The difference in my mother's and my wife's cooking is easy to explain. Just take chicken, for example. My mother made it basically one way then, when I was growing up. My wife will make chicken 400 different ways!

I know that I joke all the time about Pam's cooking: "What does my wife make? She makes reservations!" But Pam is an *excellent* cook. I just don't give her much chance to cook for me when I'm home.

You see, I'm usually home for such short stretches that I don't want her to spend hours fussing over a fancy meal—then more time afterwards while we clean up the kitchen.

So, I take her and the kids out to eat—even for some holiday meals. Hey, the important thing is that we are all *together*, enjoying each other to the fullest, whether we're at home or at a restaurant.

Some of Pam's recipes are included at the end of this chapter, in a section entitled "A Feast of Friends." Coach V says, be sure to check out her pot roast recipe; it's one my Mom just had to have the first time she tasted it. And Pam has swapped other recipes with Mom, too.

My Mom has, of course, tried to teach Pam how to make all my favorite Italian dishes, but she can't make them taste *exactly* the same. (Pam swears my Mom has some kind of "oil" in her fingertips that's the missing secret ingredient. Maybe that's true, but Mom has made an extra-special effort to write down *everything*—every ingredient, every measurement, every step—for the recipes she sent us for this book. And then she tested every one herself to make sure you can achieve similar results by following her directions. Remember, it helps to buy your ingredients from an Italian butcher or grocer.)

The dinner I have chosen to spotlight Pam's talents in the kitchen is not fancy, but it is very special to me because it is the one Pam prepared for our first meal as a married couple, just moved into our very own apartment. It's got pork chops the way I love them. (I like them best cooked with cream of mushroom soup and scalloped potatoes.) And I love the green bean casserole, too. This is "a sentimental supper" for me. So that's what we call it.

HOT WHITE CLAM DIP

8 ounces cream cheese, softened
1 can minced clams, drained
½ cup milk
1 teaspoon horseradish
Dash onion salt
Dash garlic salt

Combine all ingredients, blending well. Bake in preheated 350-degree oven 15 minutes covered, 10 minutes uncovered. Stir. Serve with large corn chips.

SUPER SALAD

3 tablespoons sugar
1 teaspoon salt
Dash freshly ground pepper
Dash of Accent
¼ cup salad oil
3½ teaspoons wine vinegar
Lettuce, shredded
½ medium onion, thinly sliced
½ cup chow mein noodles
5 slices bacon, cooked and crumbled

Combine sugar, salt, pepper, Accent, oil and vinegar several hours in advance. To serve, combine lettuce, onion, noodles and bacon. Toss well with dressing.

Note: Pam originally got this recipe from Cynthia Fletcher, the wife of one of my former assistant coaches at State. Marty Fletcher is now head basketball coach at Virginia Military Institute in Lexington, Va.

GREEN BEAN CASSEROLE

2 (10-ounce) boxes frozen french-style green beans
1 can cream of mushroom soup
1 can onion rings

Cook beans slightly, drain. Place beans in greased casserole; cover with soup. Bake in preheated 350-degree oven until hot. Remove from oven, add onion rings. Return to oven until onion rings brown slightly.

PORK CHOPS & SCALLOPED POTATOES

Potatoes, sliced
6 - 8 pork chops
2 cans cream of mushroom soup

Cover bottom of greased casserole with sliced potatoes. Cover potatoes with 1 can soup. Add pork chops. Cover chops with remaining can of soup. Bake in preheated 350-degree oven 1 hour.

CREAM CHEESE POUND CAKE

8 ounces cream cheese, softened
½ cup butter
¾ cup solid vegetable shortening
2 cups sugar
5 eggs
1 cup milk
3 cups flour
2 teaspoons vanilla

Cream cheese, butter and shortening. Add sugar and beat in eggs, 1 at a time. Alternately add flour and milk. Stir in vanilla.

Bake in preheated 325-degree oven 1¼ hours in prepared tube pan. Cool. Sprinkle with powdered sugar.

A FEAST OF FRIENDS

*The feeling of friendship is like that of
being comfortably filled with roast beef;
love, like being enlivened with champagne.*
—Samuel Johnson.

During my 18-year odyssey as an assistant or head basketball coach at six different colleges and universities, my wife Pam and I have made many, many friends, a number of whom have shared their culinary specialties with us in this section—which we naturally call "A Feast of Friends."

If friendship is truly "the wine of life," as Edward Young says, we have supped deeply of its joy and sweetness, in generous servings, wherever we have been.

This book has provided the impetus to renew "auld acquaintance" with many of these friends, and will doubtless accelerate some long-overdue reunions. And other old friends—friends of my family and friends from Pam's and my childhood—have also shared their favorite recipes.

Sharp readers will note that quite a few of my wife's recipes appear in the next few pages. Well, how could I leave out my *best friend!*

Where space permits, I have tried to say a little something about a few of the contributors who have played major roles in my life and career. Limited space simply doesn't allow me to explain *why* each and every contributor is important to my family and me. But they *know* how warmly we feel about them.

After all, the meals that we have shared together have been the "cement" that has sealed our friendship—for a lifetime.

CHEESE BALL

MAKES ONE LARGE BALL

½ pound butter, softened
3 tablespoons heavy cream, room temperature
6 ounces cream cheese, softened
1 jar pimiento cheese
1 jar pimiento cheese with olives
1 jar blue cheese
1 jar Old English cheese
1 small package Velveeta cheese
Salt
Onion powder
Walnuts, chopped

Cream butter with heavy cream. Add cheeses, salt and onion powder; blend well. Refrigerate 4 hours.

Divide and roll into large ball. Roll in chopped walnuts.

From Pam Valvano, Cary, N.C.

CHEESE BEOREG

1 pound filo dough
1/3 cup parsley, chopped
1 teaspoon baking powder
2 eggs, beaten
1 pound brick cheese, coarsely grated
½ pound butter, melted and kept warm

Mix parsley, eggs, baking powder and cheese. Set aside.

Place half of filo in 9-by-12-inch baking pan. Spread with cheese mixture. Add remaining filo. Cut very carefully into 2-inch squares. Pour warm butter over squares.

Bake in preheated 350-degree oven 20-25 minutes.

From Ardie Koehler, High Point, N.C., who says that this is an Armenian recipe that was passed down in the family.

COCKTAIL MEATBALLS

MAKES FIVE DOZEN

1 pound ground beef
½ cup dry bread crumbs
1/3 cup dehydrated onion
¼ cup milk
1 egg
1 tablespoon parsley
1 teaspoon salt
½ teaspoon pepper
½ teaspoon Worcestershire
sauce
¼ cup shortening
12 ounces chili sauce
10 ounces grape jelly

Combine beef, bread crumbs, onion, milk, egg, parsley, salt, pepper and Worcestershire sauce. Shape into small balls. Brown in melted shortening. Drain.

Heat chili sauce and jelly in saucepan, stirring until jelly melts. Add meatballs; simmer uncovered 30 minutes. Serve in fondue or chafing dish with cocktail picks.

From Pam Valvano, Cary, N.C.

PESTO SAUCE

1 cup fresh basil leaves, stems removed
¼ teaspoon black pepper
1 tablespoon pignoli nuts (pine nuts)
3 cloves garlic
1 cup olive oil
¼ cup cheese, locatelli, Romano or Parmesan, grated

Put all ingredients in blender. Blend until mixture is smooth and thin. If mixture is too thick, thin with additional oil. No cooking is necessary for sauce. Use sauce on your favorite pasta cooked as per package directions. Can be served warm or cold.

From Frank Rizzi, Merrick, N.Y.

CHEDDAR CHEESE SOUP

½ cup bacon, diced
1 tablespoon butter
¾ cup carrots, sliced thin
1 cup onion, chopped
1 cup celery, sliced thin
¾ cup sweet red pepper,
chopped
3 cups chicken stock
1½ cups beer
3½ cups milk
1 pound sharp cheddar cheese,
shredded
2/3 cup flour
½ cup heavy cream
Salt and pepper to taste
Parsley, chopped

Melt butter in frying pan. Add bacon and cook until crisp and brown. Remove from pan, drain on paper towel and set aside.

Add vegetables to frying pan and sauté in bacon drippings until onion is transparent. Stir occasionally. Add vegetables to soup pot with stock and beer. Bring to boil; simmer until vegetables are tender.

Scald milk over medium heat. Place cheese and flour in plastic bag. Shake to combine. Add cheese/flour mixture to hot milk. Cook until cheese melts and mixture thickens, stirring constantly. Add this mixture and cream to soup pot. Season to taste with salt and pepper. Heat through. Garnish with bacon and parsley.

From Ginny and Dee Rowe, Storrs, Conn. (Dee was head basketball coach at the University of Connecticut when I was an assistant coach there.)

PASTA

ITALIAN PASTA SALAD

½ box small pasta shells,
cooked
¼ pound hard salami, cut up
¼ pound provolone cheese,
cut up
¼ pound pepperoni, sliced
1 green pepper, diced
1 small onion, chopped
2 ripe tomatoes, chopped
1 rib celery, chopped
½ jar stuffed green olives

¾ cup olive oil
½ cup vinegar
1 tablespoon oregano
1½ teaspoons salt
½ teaspoon pepper

Mix all ingredients together. Marinate in dressing overnight.

DRESSING

Combine all ingredients and pour over pasta mixture.

From Joan Miller, Lewisburg, Pa.

PASTA E FAGIOLI

SERVES SIX PEOPLE

2 cups Great Northern beans,
soaked overnight in water
8 cups fresh water
2½ (16-ounce) cans stewed
tomatoes
Smoked ham bone, salt pork,
pork skin, prosciutto or
smoked shoulder
Salt and pepper
Pinch of sugar
Pasta

Drain beans. Put in fresh water. Add tomatoes and meat. Simmer slowly until beans are soft but firm, about 3 hours. Add more water if needed.

Season to taste with salt, pepper, pinch of sugar.

Five minutes before serving, add pasta to boiling soup.

From Josephine A. Cestaro, Long Island, N.Y.

BARBECUE BRISKET

SERVES 10 PEOPLE

1 (10-12 pound) beef brisket
1 large onion, sliced
1 lemon, sliced
2 cups ketchup
2 cups water
2 tablespoons liquid smoke
2 tablespoons Worcestershire
sauce
1 teaspoon mustard
4 tablespoons brown sugar
1 teaspoon salt

Place brisket in shallow baking pan. Place onion and lemon slices on top of brisket. Wrap in aluminum foil.

Bake in 250-degree oven 6-8 hours. Remove foil. Slice thinly after discarding lemon, onion and fat. Place slices in baking dish and cover with sauce. Bake in 300-degree oven 30-45 minutes.

To prepare sauce, combine ketchup, water, liquid smoke, Worcestershire sauce, mustard, brown sugar and salt. Bring to boil over high heat. Remove from heat.

From Doris Mueller, Houston, Texas

CHICKEN MARSALA

1½ pounds boned chicken
2 medium onions
1 tablespoon butter
1½ tablespoons vegetable oil
2 cloves garlic, crushed
3 teaspoons mushroom soy sauce or regular soy sauce
3 cups tomato juice
1 cup Marsala wine
⅛ teaspoon pepper
⅛ teaspoon sugar
¼ teaspoon carraway seeds
1 carrot, sliced
1 stalk celery, sliced
2 tablespoons flour
1 (16-ounce) package noodles

Cut chicken into cubes and put in bowl with soy sauce. Chop onions and sauté in butter about 5 minutes. Put in bowl.

Heat vegetable oil and fry chicken few pieces at a time. Add garlic and sauté. Pour in any leftover soy sauce.

When all of chicken seems light and hard to touch, add 2 cups of tomato juice and wine to skillet. Add pepper, sugar and carraway seeds. Add carrot and celery, stir. Cover and let simmer for 1½ hours.

Mix 2 tablespoons flour with remaining cup of tomato juice. Add to skillet and mix. Let simmer for additional 30 minutes, stirring occasionally.

Boil 3 quarts of water, adding dash of oil, in 4-quart pot. When water boils, add noodles. Follow directions on package but do not overcook.

Serve chicken over noodles.

This may also be served with rice. It is excellent for goulash lovers who are not supposed to eat red meat.

From Buster Wolosky, Seaford, N.Y.

CHICKEN PARMESAN

SERVES SIX PEOPLE

½ stick butter
1 clove garlic, minced
1 cup seasoned bread crumbs
1 cup Parmesan cheese, grated
1 teaspoon salt
⅛ teaspoon pepper
Parsley, chopped
6 boneless chicken breasts

Melt butter, add garlic and simmer. Mix crumbs, cheese and seasonings. Dip chicken in butter mixture, roll in cheese and crumbs. Place in pan. Bake at 350 degrees for ½ hour, then 300 degrees for another ½ hour.

CHICKEN PARMESAN SALTA IN BOCCA

SERVES SIX PEOPLE

This is a variation of the above.

Pound chicken breasts. Add thin slices of ham, sliced mozzarella cheese and chopped tomatoes. Sprinkle on pinch of sage. Roll and follow directions above.

From Kay Lloyd, Los Altos Hills, Calif. (Kay is the wife of my college roommate, Bob Lloyd.)

CHICKEN REUBEN

SERVES FOUR PEOPLE

4 chicken breasts
1 can sauerkraut, drained
1 can mushrooms, drained, or
6 medium-sized fresh
4 slices Swiss cheese
1 jar Thousand Island salad
dressing

Place chicken in greased baking dish. Layer remaining ingredients over chicken in order listed.

Bake, covered, in preheated 300-degree oven for 1½ hours.

From Pam Valvano, Cary, N.C.

COUNTRY CAPTAIN

SERVES SIX PEOPLE

2 chickens, 2½ pounds each,
cut in pieces
¼ cup flour
2 teaspoons salt
½ teaspoon pepper
3 tablespoons oil
1 large onion, chopped
1 large green pepper, chopped
1 clove garlic
3 teaspoons curry powder
1 pound can tomatoes
½ cup raisins

Combine flour, 1 teaspoon salt, ¼ teaspoon pepper. Coat chicken with flour mixture, broil chicken until brown.

Sauté onion, green pepper, garlic and curry powder in oil. Add tomatoes, salt, pepper, raisins. Add chicken. Simmer 1 hour.

From Pam Valvano, Cary, N.C.

CREAMED CUTLETS

SERVES SIX PEOPLE

10 chicken breasts, deboned
1 can cream of chicken soup
½ pint sour cream
½ cup cooking sherry

Place chicken breasts in greased baking dish.

Combine remaining ingredients, pour over chicken, sprinkle with paprika.

Bake uncovered in preheated 375-degree oven 45 minutes or until top dries slightly and turns golden.

From Pam Valvano, Cary, N.C.

CREOLE SHRIMP

SERVES SIX PEOPLE

5 pounds shrimp in the shell
(large shrimp are best)
1 large bottle Italian dressing
1 pound butter
½ cup lemon juice
Worcestershire sauce
Tabasco
Garlic salt
Pepper (be liberal in usage)

Place unpeeled shrimp in large baking pan. Pour dressing and lemon juice over shrimp. Cut butter into small pieces, scattering over shrimp. Sprinkle mixture with seasoning. When melted, liquid should just about cover shrimp.

Bake in preheated 300-degree oven for about 1 hour, turning frequently.

Serve with salad and ample garlic bread to dip into the sauce used in cooking shrimp. Provide plenty of napkins.

From my mother-in-law, Wilma Levine, Winter Park, Fla.

MINUTE STEAK SCRAMBLE

SERVES FOUR PEOPLE

4 cube steaks, cut in julienne strips
¼ teaspoon garlic salt
¼ teaspoon ginger
¼ cup salad oil
2 green peppers, cut in julienne strips
1 cup celery, cut in pieces diagonally
1 tablespoon cornstarch
¼ cup cold water
3 tablespoons soy sauce
2 tomatoes, cut in wedges

Season meat with garlic salt and ginger. Heat half of oil in skillet; add meat and brown quickly. Remove meat, add remaining oil, then pepper and celery. Cook until slightly tender (about 3 minutes).

Mix together cornstarch, water and soy sauce. Add to skillet, cook until thick. Add meat and tomatoes and heat well. Serve with rice.

From Pam Valvano, Cary, N.C.

MUSSELS IN MARINARA SAUCE

SERVES FOUR PEOPLE

3 cloves of garlic, chopped
3 tablespoons olive oil
1 pound can whole crushed tomatoes
3 pounds mussels
Fresh basil (optional)
Oregano (optional)

Soak mussels in clean fresh water overnight. This will enable mussels to rinse themselves of any sand. Add bread crumbs and/or flour to water to help mussels cleanse themselves.

Place olive oil and garlic in large pot. Brown garlic slightly. Add mussels and cover to allow them to steam open. Add tomatoes. Once tomatoes start to boil, lower heat and simmer 1 hour.

For fra diavolo, add crushed red pepper to taste. For extra zest, add basil and oregano to taste. Serve as appetizer or main dish over spaghetti or linguine.

From Frank Rizzi, Merrick, N.Y.

POT ROAST

4½-pound brisket of beef
4 carrots
3 ribs celery
3 onions, thickly sliced
1 bay leaf
Salt
Pepper
Paprika
4 cubes beef bouillon
3 cups water
1 cup ketchup

Place roast in uncovered pan. Cook in preheated 400-degree oven 30 minutes or until brown.

Add carrots, celery, onions, bay leaf, salt, pepper, paprika. Dissolve bouillon cubes in water. Combine with ketchup and add to roast with vegetables. Cover.

Cook in 350-degree oven 2½ hours or until tender. Slice meat and put back into gravy to serve.

From Pam Valvano, Cary, N.C.

SOUR MEAT

2 cups vinegar
4 cups water
8 whole cloves
3 bay leaves
6 onions
1 clove garlic
12 whole peppercorns
12 whole allspice
5 pound rump roast
2 tablespoons oil
12 gingersnaps

Brown meat in oil. Add onions and brown. Add rest of ingredients. Simmer until tender, 3-4 hours. Thicken gravy with gingersnaps dissolved in cold water. Add more if desired.

From Gladys Giacalone, Seaford, N.Y.

STROMBOLI

1 pound pizza dough
(homemade or from pizza
parlor)
¼ cup flour
8 ounces fried onions and
peppers (sold in jars)
8 ounces mozzarella cheese
½ pound prosciutto
½ pound pepperoni

Sprinkle wooden board with flour. Cut dough in half. Roll each half into rectangle about 4 by 8 inches.

Drain onions and peppers. Dry. Slice mozzarella into pieces about size of pepperoni.

Starting from left, about ½ inch from end, put piece of pepperoni. Overlap with piece of prosciutto. Overlap that with a piece of mozzarella. Continue to within 1 inch of end of dough. Spread on onions and peppers.

Roll up jelly-roll fashion. Pinch seams closed. Pinch ends closed. A little water will help close seams if necessary. Repeat with rest of dough and ingredients.

Bake on foil in preheated 400-degree oven for about 20 minutes or until dough is dark and crisp to the touch. Let cool for 10 minutes. Slice in 1- or 2-inch pieces and serve.

From Buster Wolosky, Seaford, N.Y., who says, "Although the name is Italian, I know of no Italian that uses this name for this dish. You can use any kind of sandwich meat if you aren't a pepperoni or prosciutto fan. Before you bake the Stromboli, you can sprinkle some sesame or poppy seeds on top of the dough."

SUPER EGG

2 eggs, beaten
½ cup flour
½ cup milk
¼ cup butter
Jelly
Powdered sugar

Heat oven to 425 degrees. Place butter in pie plate. Place pie plate in oven until butter melts.

Combine eggs, flour, milk and scramble in bowl. Pour mixture into pie plate on top of melted butter. Do not mix with butter.

Bake 15-20 minutes. Sides will puff out and become brown. Middle will become firm but will not rise.

Remove from oven. Sprinkle with powdered sugar. Serve with jelly.

Note: This is a light fluffy dish—sort of a cross between an omelet and a pancake. It's perfect for breakfast, brunch or an easy supper.

From Lynn Ford Flint, Tampa, Fla. (Lynn was Pam's Maid of Honor at our wedding.)

VEGETABLES

BROCCOLI & MUSHROOMS

SERVES FOUR PEOPLE

1 bunch broccoli
3 tablespoons olive oil
2 cloves garlic
Salt to taste
½ teaspoon red pepper
1 small can mushrooms

Parboil broccoli. Sauté garlic in oil. Add mushrooms, broccoli, salt and pepper. Cook 15 minutes.

From Josephine A. Cestaro, Long Island, N.Y.

POTATO BALLS

SERVES 10 PEOPLE

5 pounds cooked potatoes, riced
3 eggs
2 cups flour
Nutmeg to taste
Salt and pepper
Croutons

Mix together first 5 ingredients. Form into small balls. Push crouton into center of each. Drop carefully, 1 or 2 at a time, into pot of boiling salted water. Cook about 10 minutes. Serve with sour meat. (See recipe elsewhere in this section.)

From Gladys Giacalone, Seaford, N.Y.

POTATO PIE

3 pounds potatoes, boiled and mashed
1 egg
¼ cup cheese, locatelli, Romano or Parmesan, grated
1 tablespoon parsley, minced or chopped
½ pound mozzarella, diced
2-3 slices pepperoni or genoa salami, diced
1 cup bread crumbs (plain)
4 teaspoons butter

Thoroughly mix all ingredients together. Butter 8-inch pie plate or casserole dish and layer with bread crumbs. Place mixture in prepared pie plate. Top with remaining bread crumbs and butter.

Bake in preheated 425-degree oven 30 minutes. Makes excellent side dish.

From Frank Rizzi, Merrick, N.Y.

ZUCCHINI CASSEROLE

Zucchini, sliced
Onion, sliced
Tomato, sliced
Longhorn cheddar cheese, grated
Parmesan cheese, grated

Layer vegetables and cheese in greased casserole in desired amount, ending with cheese. Sprinkle Parmesan over top. Cover with foil. Bake in preheated 350-degree oven 60 minutes.

From Pam Valvano, Cary. N.C. (This is one of my all-time favorites.)

SALADS

BROCCOLI-MUSHROOM SALAD

1 pound fresh mushrooms
Florets of 1 head of broccoli
2 green onions, finely chopped

Mix ingredients in salad bowl. Serve with dressing.

DRESSING

½ cup fine sugar
1 teaspoon salt
1 teaspoon paprika
1 teaspoon celery seed or celery salt
1 teaspoon onion powder
¼ cup cider or wine vinegar
1 cup oil

Mix ingredients in wide-mouth jar, shake and let sit for 1 hour. Pour over salad and leave for 30 minutes. Stir and wait another 30 minutes before serving.

From Lynn Ford Flint, Tampa, Fla.

LEMON-BLUEBERRY SALAD

3 ounces lemon gelatin
3 ounces blackberry gelatin
1 cup boiling water
½ cup cold water
1 tablespoon lemon juice
1 (21-ounce) can blueberry pie filling
¼ cup powdered sugar
1 cup sour cream

Mix gelatin with boiling water, add lemon juice and cold water. Stir in pie filling. Pour into an 8-by-8-by-2-inch dish. Chill until firm.

Blend sour cream with powdered sugar, spread over gelatin. Cut to serve.

From Pam Valvano, Cary, N.C.

DESSERT-LIKE SALAD

6 ounces lemon gelatin
3¾ cups boiling water
3 tablespoons sugar
3 apples, chopped
2 bananas, cut fine
1 (#2) can crushed pineapple, drained

Dissolve gelatin and sugar in boiling water. Let cool until slightly thick.

Add apples, bananas and crushed pineapple. Chill until firm. Spread with topping.

TOPPING

½ cup pineapple juice
¼ cup sugar
1 tablespoon flour
1 egg, beaten
1 envelope powdered whipped topping mix

Combine juice, sugar, flour and egg; cook until thick, stirring constantly. Cool.

Fold in whipped topping prepared according to package. Spread over gelatin, 1 hour before serving. Cut to serve.

From Pam Valvano, Cary, N.C.

POTATO SALAD

15 large potatoes
1 cup sugar
1 egg
6 teaspoons cornstarch
½ teaspoon salt
1 cup water
1/3 cup vinegar
1 tablespoon mustard
1½ cups celery, chopped
1 hard-boiled egg
Salt
Parsley
3 tablespoons mayonnaise

Cook potatoes in peel. Skin, cut into slices.

Combine sugar, egg, cornstarch, salt, water, vinegar and mustard in saucepan and bring to boil. Cook, stirring constantly, until thick.

Remove from heat. Add mayonnaise, beat with mixer.

Add celery, egg, salt and parsley to potatoes. Pour cooked dressing over potatoes, tossing to coat. Refrigerate.

From Pam Valvano, Cary, N.C.

POTATO SALAD DRESSING

1 egg, beaten
½ cup sugar
½ cup water
½ cup vinegar
1 tablespoon flour
2 tablespoons butter
½ teaspoon salt
¼ teaspoon pepper
Dash turmeric and mustard
3 tablespoons mayonnaise

Combine ingredients in order given except for mayonnaise.

Boil until thick, stirring continuously. Cool in refrigerator.

Stir in mayonnaise and pour over potatoes which have been boiled and diced.

From Judy Lebda, Lewisburg, Pa.

BREADS & BEVERAGES

CORN FRITTERS

MAKES 18-20

½ cup canned corn
1 egg
1/3 cup sugar
2½ cups dry pancake mix
Vegetable oil
Powdered sugar

Mix ingredients, using enough pancake mix to make biscuit-like texture. Heat enough oil to deep fry to 375 degrees. Fry until golden brown. Sprinkle with sugar.

From Josephine A. Cestaro, Long Island, N.Y.

KAHLUA

2 cups water
4 cups sugar
2 ounces Italian instant espresso
4 cups vodka
1 vanilla bean

Bring water to boil, add espresso to half of water. Add sugar and remaining water, stir well until all ingredients dissolve. Cool.

Add vodka, mix well. Pour into dark half-gallon bottles, with screw lids. Break vanilla bean into small pieces, add to bottles. Seal. Let stand for 30 days or longer. Shake weekly until ready.

From Pam Valvano, Cary, N.C.

DESSERTS

CHOCOLATE SAUCE

1 cup sugar
2 tablespoons cocoa
2 tablespoons margarine
1 small can evaporated milk
1 teaspoon vanilla

Combine sugar and cocoa. Add margarine and blend. Add milk, stirring constantly while cooking over medium heat. Increase heat and bring to boil for 1 minute, stirring constantly. Remove from heat.

Add vanilla; blend well. Cool. Serve over ice cream.

From Ruth Stewart, Greenwood, S.C. (Ruth is the mother of Dick Stewart, a long-time friend, and my business manager.)

CREAM CHEESE BROWNIES

8 ounces sweet chocolate
5 tablespoons butter
3 ounces cream cheese
1 cup sugar
3 eggs
Salt
½ cup flour
1½ teaspoons vanilla
½ teaspoon baking powder
9-by-9 inch baking pan, greased

Melt butter and chocolate together. Set aside. Cream cheese and sugar until smooth. Add flour, baking powder, vanilla to cheese and mix until smooth. Beat in eggs. Pour batter into prepared baking dish. Pour chocolate mixture into batter and swirl chocolate through. Bake in preheated 350-degree oven 35-40 minutes. Cool and cut into squares. squares.

From Lynn Ford Flint, Tampa, Fla.

CREAM CHEESE TARTS

MAKES 48

6 ounces cream cheese, softened
2 sticks butter, softened
1 cup flour
1 cup sugar
2 eggs, separated
1 cup golden raisins
1 cup pecans, chopped
2 teaspoons vanilla
Powdered sugar

Combine cream cheese, 1 stick butter and flour. Spread each muffin tin cup with mixture to create lining. Refrigerate 1 hour.

Mix sugar, remaining butter, egg yolks, raisins, pecans and vanilla.

Beat egg whites until stiff, then fold into mixture. Spoon into each muffin cup until half filled.

Bake in preheated 350-degree oven 25-30 minutes. Remove from oven and sprinkle with powdered sugar.

From Millie Occhiuto, New Rochelle, N.Y.

MANDELBRAT

3 eggs
¾ cup oil
1 cup sugar
1 teaspoon vanilla
¼ cup rum
3 cups flour
1 cup nuts, chopped
2 teaspoons baking powder

Beat together eggs, oil, sugar, vanilla and rum. Add flour, nuts, baking powder. Blend well.

Form into 3 strips with wet hands. Lay out strips on baking sheet.

Bake in preheated 300-degree oven 30 minutes. Cut in slices, lay on side, return to oven for 15 minutes.

From Rose Lichtenstein, Seaford, N.Y.

PASSOVER SPONGE CAKE

9 eggs, separated
1½ cups sugar
½ cup cake flour
¼ cup potato flour
1 lemon
½ orange
1 cup nuts, chopped (optional)

Beat egg yolks with sugar. Add flour.

Juice orange and lemon and grate rinds of both. Add juice and rind to egg mixture.

Beat egg whites until stiff and fold into egg yolk mixture. Add nuts if desired.

Bake in preheated 350-degree oven 1 hour in springform pan. Turn upside down to cool.

From Rose Lichtenstein, Seaford, N.Y.

PEPPERMINT BONBON DESSERT

½ box vanilla wafers, crushed
¼ cup butter, melted
2/3 cup butter
2 cups powdered sugar
2 ounces unsweetened chocolate, melted
3 egg yolks, beaten
1 teaspoon vanilla
½ cup walnuts, chopped
3 egg whites, beaten stiff
1 quart chocolate chip mint ice cream, softened

Combine ¼ cup melted butter with crumbs, press into 9-by-13-inch pan and freeze.

Combine remaining butter, sugar, chocolate, egg yolks and vanilla, beating well. Stir in walnuts. Fold in egg whites.

Spread mixture over crumbs. Freeze. Add ice cream. Freeze. Cut to serve.

From Pam Valvano, Cary, N.C.

RICOTTA PUDDING CAKE

1 package yellow pudding
cake mix
2 pounds ricotta cheese,
room temperature
2 teaspoons vanilla
4 eggs
¾ cup sugar

Mix cake according to package directions. Pour into greased and floured 9-by-13-by-2-inch cake pan.

Combine cheese, vanilla, eggs and sugar and pour over batter.

Bake in preheated 350-degree oven 1 hour. Sprinkle with powdered sugar.

From Rose Lichtenstein, Seaford, N.Y.

SWEDISH APPLE PIE

4 large Rome Beauty apples,
sliced
1½ tablespoons cinnamon
Lemon juice
1 cup butter
1½ cups sugar
2 eggs
1½ cups flour
¾ cup walnuts, chopped

Place apples in ungreased springform pan. Mix remaining ingredients, spread over apples, pat in place.

Bake in preheated 350-degree oven 1 hour, 10 minutes.

Place tinfoil under pan to catch drippings.

From Rose Lichtenstein, Seaford, N.Y.

STRAWBERRY PIE

CRUST

1½ cups flour
2 tablespoons sugar
½ teaspoon salt
2 tablespoons milk
½ cup vegetable oil

Mix all together until you have oily ball. Press into 8-inch pie plate. Do not roll. Bake 15 minutes in preheated 400-degree oven or until light brown.

FILLING

1 cup sugar
3 tablespoons cornstarch
1 tablespoon white corn syrup
1 cup water
Few drops red food color
3 tablespoons strawberry gelatin (dry)
1 quart hulled strawberries

Stir together sugar, cornstarch and gelatin. Add rest of ingredients, except strawberries. Bring mixture to a boil and cook until thick. Set aside and let cool. When cool, add strawberries. Stir to coat and pour into baked pie shell. Refrigerate for a few hours. Top with whipped cream.

From Ginny and Dee Rowe, Storrs, Conn.

THE WORLD'S BEST BARBECUE

Let's talk Southern.

That means let's talk barbecue.

When I came to N.C. State in 1980, the Wolfpackers wanted me to feel at home. They figured that the way to do that was to feed me the pride of good old-fashioned Southern food—good old North Carolina barbecue.

They thought I'd never had it before and that it was their patriotic duty to make sure I got a chance to see what had been keeping these Southern boys (and girls) happy and feisty all these years.

So when I started the Wolfpack Tour that spring, I'd go to a place, and they'd say, "Jim, in honor of your being here today, we have barbecue for you." That was great.

Then I'd go to the next place, and they'd say, "Jim, in honor of your being here today, we have barbecue for you."

Fine.

They'd fill up my plate, and I'd do like a little kid does when he's got something he's not sure he likes. I'd eat it all up very fast. Then they'd breathe a sigh of relief—and give me another plate full.

The first place I ever had North Carolina barbecue was at Wilber's Barbecue and Restaurant in Goldsboro. And I know that Wilber Shirley says that when I first got here from New York, I didn't know barbecue from little green apples. But honestly, folks, I did. After all, little green apples *are* green, and barbecue is various shades of brown—depending on what part of the country you're in.

During my first month in North Carolina, March 1980, I must have spoken to at least 42 luncheons and dinners as part of the Wolfpack Club's spring tour—and it seems like I had barbecue all 42 times. Consequently, during the whole month of April, I was frequently afflicted with what we Southerners call "the green-apple quickstep." (See, Wilber, barbecue and those little green apples may have more in common than you think.)

Anyway, that's the story I told then—and have been telling ever since. And when it got into the media, the barbecue lovers banded together and started feeding me everything but barbecue. They gave me chicken. They gave me roast beef. They even gave me linguine with white clam sauce. Now they hardly ever give me barbecue.

Come on, folks. I was only kidding. I love the stuff.

There's a saying that in the East, barbecue is pork; in Texas, it's beef; and in California, it's a verb.

And in New York, where I come from, it's a noun—as in backyard barbecue. When you tell people to come over for a barbecue, you mean hot dogs and hamburgers on the grill.

I still cook things on the grill. Whenever I have recruits down, I grill burgers for them. I go around and ask everybody how he'd like his: rare, medium, well-done. Then I cook them all the same way—burnt.

But now I know barbecue isn't really a noun.

I've gotten a Southern education.

It wasn't easy. I mean, I used to think a pig pickin' was a wild weekend. When they told me we were going to something by that name, I said, "Yeah, we used to have those in college, but we didn't advertise them like you do down here."

Now I understand that a pig pickin' is taking barbecue back to basics. Nothing between you and the meat except your fingers.

I love to step up there and rip off big slabs.

I've also learned that barbecue is one of North Carolina's more controversial subjects. Eaters arguing over how to make it or where to get it can get madder than a basketball player who's just been mugged, tripped and stomped on without drawing a foul.

I found out what a serious subject this is when I went to Wilber's. Even though it was the first time I'd had barbecue, naturally I expressed myself in my usual mild-mannered way and pronounced Wilber's the best barbecue in the state. That set off a whole avalanche of protests, because everybody said, "Now wait a minute."

When I got to Lexington, they presented me with an entire shoulder of barbecue just to show me how wrong I was. We were on the road three or four days, and we had to lug this shoulder around with us everywhere we went.

And when I got up in the mountains to North Wilkesboro, they told me THEY had the best barbecue.

I couldn't argue with them, 'cause, heck, I liked it all.

I'm a modest enough man to admit that a few years in the South isn't enough to qualify me as a barbecue expert. You practically have to be born in a pit and spend your childhood sprinkling on hot sauce to get that kind of expertise.

You've got to understand the earth-shaking differences between using the whole pig or part of it. You gotta understand the ketchup question — does it or doesn't it belong in the sauce? Even the slaw (to mayonnaise or not to mayonnaise) is a hot issue.

So in the interests of good eating, I asked two of the state's better-known barbecue bards to share their knowledge with me. Read Jerry Bledsoe's and Dennis Rogers' opinions and judge for yourself.

Just remember that man does not live by barbecue alone; he must have hush puppies, cornbread or cornsticks, cole slaw and potato salad.

Here's what Jerry — a columnist for *The Greensboro Daily News* — has to say.

"I'm real hard on people who don't face up to the facts and tell the truth about barbecue.

"In North Carolina, there are two styles — Western (it's also called Lexington) and Eastern. They vary in sauces and the way the cooking is done. Eastern does whole split pigs, and Western does just the shoulders. They even have a different cole slaw — yellow or white slaw for the East and red slaw for the West.

"When you have a genuine barbecue from the East, you don't have to argue over which one is better. They're equal. But the trouble is, in the East you have practically no barbecue left. All the major places have gone to cooking with gas or electricity. That doesn't give you barbecue. It gives you roast pork.

"The whole idea of barbecue is to cook meat over hot wood coals and get the wood flavor into the meat. In the East, you get all these little things in your mouth and wonder what the hell they are. They're ground-up skin. That's the only way they have to give the meat any flavor. So what you're getting is roast pork and ground skin with a little vinegar and hot peppers and salt on it.

"Dennis Rogers will take you down East, but that man has never tasted real barbecue to my knowledge. He goes to these gas-fired places and thinks that's barbecue.

"Probably the best in the East is Wilber's in Goldsboro. It's a superb barbecue place. And there's a place in Kinston, the Barbecue Lodge, that does a good job.

"But the West has Lexington, the barbecue center of the world. There is no other place like it on earth. It has 18 barbecue restaurants for a population of something like 18,000 and almost all of them do it right. They cook it over wood — primarily hickory if they can get it. They do it right, and that's why they have the reputation they have and so many people come there.

"Lexington is what makes North Carolina barbecue superior.

"Out in Texas and Kansas, they use beef and it doesn't take the smoking the way pork does. Beef doesn't absorb the flavor the same and isn't as enhanced by the wood smoke. It's as if God himself had decreed there would be barbecue and designed pork for that purpose.

"Even in Florida or Mississippi or Georgia or South Carolina, where they often use pork and cook it over wood, they slap on these heavy, overbearing sauces and ooze them all over to the point all you are tasting is sauce.

"North Carolina sauces are designed specially to lightly enhance the flavor of the meat. They don't take away the wood-smoked flavor. North Carolina lucked out. They had some geniuses here in the old days — and they still have some today.

"In Western North Carolina, the sauce is just salt, sugar, distilled vinegar, water, ketchup, black pepper and, sometimes, a touch of ground or crushed red pepper. They use the same sauce for the meat as they do for the slaw (that's why it's red). It's just that simple.

"In Lexington, you can hardly miss, whichever restaurant you choose. Lexington No. 1 is the best in the state.   That's Wayne Monk's place. He's the one who cooked for President Reagan and the heads of state at the summit meeting in Williamsburg. And Smoky Joe's, the Barbecue Center, Jimmy's, Speedy's — any of those are going to be good places."

Thanks, Jerry. Now here's what Dennis Rogers — columnist for *The (Raleigh) News and Observer* — thinks. Dennis, by the way, admits to being the world's foremost expert on the Holy Grub and urges us not to forget that barbecue is a cultural, social and almost religious experience.

"If you are looking for good barbecue, you need look no further than Eastern North Carolina. In fact, if you are looking for barbecue at all, you MUST look no further than Eastern North Carolina. When I am hankering for a big piece of dead hog meat with tomato sauce, I like to follow the advice of my good friend Jerry Bledsoe and head West where you find lots of it. For some silly reason, Jerry calls THAT barbecue, but it wouldn't fool even a good Italian boy from Queens, much less native-born barbecue gluttons.

"For barbecue the way it was meant to be — tender, succulent, vinegar sharp and heavenly smooth — Eastern North Carolina offers an almost unlimited range of eateries.

"Here are some of my favorite places where you can find the food that has made US justly famous (and Jerry Bledsoe jealous).

"Don Murray's in Raleigh, Bill's Barbecue in Wilson and Doug Sauls in Nashville all have great pig and my favorite side dishes: Brunswick stew, boiled potatoes, slaw and cornsticks.

"Wilber's in Goldsboro offers the traditional wood-smoked flavor and is a favorite for beachgoers. The out-of-the-way Skyline Restaurant in Ayden is one of the state's oldest and best and beats everybody with its slab cornbread.

"Even folks who work in downtown Raleigh get good barbecue at Clyde Cooper's. I especially like the chunky style."

Who's right? In the interests of scientific analysis, you'd best do your own taste test. After all, as no less a gourmet than Craig Claiborne of *The New York Times* has said, "To an experienced North Carolina barbecue addict, the differences in the Lexington and down East versions might be obvious and pronounced. To me they were slight and subtle, the main one being the sauce ingredients. And even there, the absence of a slight tomato tang in the down East sauce didn't make a whole lot of difference — vinegar is the key factor in both of them."

To give you a representative sample of North Carolina's world's-best barbecue, I asked Wayne Monk of Lexington No. 1 and Wilber Shirley of Wilber's Barbecue and Restaurant to share some of their secret recipes.

Monk, who teaches a two-week commercial cooking course on the ABCs of operating your own barbecue restaurant, was understandably reluctant to have his entire menu published. But he has contributed the recipe for his famous barbecue slaw.

BARBECUE SLAW

4 cups cabbage, chopped
¼ cup sugar
½ teaspoon black pepper
Dash ground red pepper
1 teaspoon salt
1/3 cup ketchup
2 tablespoons distilled vinegar

Combine sugar, cabbage, salt and pepper. Do not allow cabbage to get warm. Combine ketchup and vinegar. Add to cabbage mixture and mix well. Refrigerate at least 1 hour.

To sample the rest of Wayne Monk's mouth-watering menu of chopped or sliced pork barbecue, cole slaw, french fries and hush puppies, you'll have to visit Lexington No. 1, a cozy, informal place located at 10 U.S. Highway 29-70 South in Lexington. You out-of-staters can call 704/249-9814 for directions. North Carolinians *know.*

As for the proprietor of maybe *the* barbecue Mecca of the East, Wilber Shirley was more than happy to adapt some of his featured selections to the portions needed for a dinner for four. You'll notice, though, that directions are given for cooking the barbecue pork in the oven — which is what most folks will likely do.

However, if you insist on authenticity right down to the last minute detail, you can try following Wilber's directions for preparing the pork with salt and apple cider vinegar, placing the shoulder in a preheated 500-degree oven and baking it for 10 minutes exactly. Then you reduce the temperature to 275-degrees and bake 5 hours, turning the shoulder once each hour.

After oven-baking, you can wood-smoke the pork by grilling it in a barbecue cooker or on a preheated charcoal grill, laying a couple of oak or hickory sticks on the coals to impart the desired flavor. Then you cook the shoulder about 10 minutes at the lowest heat possible, scraping away the coals directly beneath the meat if you can. Just be careful that you don't let the coals or wood flame up while the meat is being smoked.

Either way you cook it — and any way you chop or slice it — Wilber's barbecue pork is something very special. And so is the rest of the typical barbecue dinner presented here. At his down-home restaurant, Wilber Shirley supplements these dishes with barbecue chicken, baked beans, cornsticks, potatoes boiled in a hot sauce (like Texas Pete), a variety of fresh-cooked vegetables and cakes.

Those who want to visit this celebrated barbecue emporium can find it on U.S. Highway 70 east of Goldsboro. You can call 919/778-5218 for directions. Tell them Coach V sent you.

WILBER'S BARBECUE DINNER

BARBECUED PORK

3-pound pork shoulder
Salt
Apple cider vinegar

Rub salt lightly over shoulder; baste lightly with vinegar. Place in roasting pan with 1 inch of water in bottom. Cover with lid or aluminum foil, and cook 5-5½ hours in preheated 450-degree oven. To tell if shoulder is done, take hold of shank end of bone. When bone is loose, shoulder is cooked all the way through.

Remove meat from pan, and chop with cleaver or slice thin. (Pork can be chopped coarse or fine, according to preference.)

Pour barbecue sauce over meat.

BARBECUE SAUCE

1½ cups apple cider vinegar
½ cup water
2 tablespoons crushed red pepper
2 tablespoons ground red pepper
1 teaspoon black pepper
½ teaspoon salt

Combine all ingredients in small saucepan, stir well and bring to boil. Remove from heat, and let cool. Spoon sauce over chopped or sliced pork. (Recipe yields enough sauce for approximately 3 pounds of chopped pork.)

COLE SLAW

1 small cabbage, about 1 pound
¾ cup salad dressing
2 tablespoons sugar
1 tablespoon mustard
1 tablespoon vinegar

Remove outer leaves and core of cabbage. Cut head in half and shred fine. Coarsely chop shreds.

Add salad dressing, sugar, mustard and vinegar. Mix well, and chill before serving.

POTATO SALAD

3 medium potatoes, peeled
½ cup salad dressing
1 teaspoon sugar
¼ cup salad cubes
2 hard-boiled eggs, chopped
(optional)

Boil and mash potatoes. Add remaining ingredients, blend thoroughly and chill before serving.

Note: For special occasions, Wilber adds two hard-boiled eggs, chopped.

HUSH PUPPIES

1 (32-ounce) bag of self-rising yellow hush puppy mix
Water
Vegetable shortening

For each 15-25 hush puppies desired, combine 1 cup mix with 2/3 cup water, and mix thoroughly. (If needed, add more water to make medium-thick batter.) Allow batter to set 3-5 minutes, then restir.

Heat vegetable shortening to 350-degrees.

Drop mixture by spoonfuls into fat, and cook until golden brown on all sides. Drain on paper towels, and serve hot.

Note: Where hush puppy mix is not available, the editors recommend combining 2 cups self-rising yellow cornmeal, 1 egg and 1¼ cup water (or buttermilk). Mix thoroughly, allow batter to set 3-5 minutes, then restir. Cook as above.

DOWN-HOME SOUTHERN COOKING

Despite evidence to the contrary, barbecue isn't all there is to Southern food.

When I think Southern food, I think plentiful. Maybe that's one reason I feel right at home whenever I sit down at a down-home meal. Like the Italians, Southerners go along with the more-the-better philosophy. None of this dainty, delicate stuff that wouldn't fill up a baby. Southern food is hefty, solid, stick-to-your ribs.

All that lard and butter and cream may not be exactly what the doctor recommends, but we all have to indulge sometimes, and if you've got a few calories to splurge, you can't spend them better than on this kind of food.

A real Southern meal probably has a fried chicken or two and a country ham just for starters. It has so many vegetables you can't count them all—corn, butterbeans, squash, tomatoes, mashed potatoes, etc., etc. And all the vegetables preferably have never traveled farther than from your garden to your table. You have biscuits; you have cornbread; you have salads.

When it's dessert time, nobody expects you to take just ONE. You get chess pie and coconut cake and peach cobbler and homemade ice cream, all piled up on the plate together. Southerners are pleased, not offended, when a visitor has a hearty appetite.

I thought I knew what iced tea was. But iced tea here is different—sweeter and stronger. Southerners drink so much of it, they have to have pitchers on the table so they can take lots of swigs and wash down the rest of the meal.

I'd never had grits until I came South. They remind me of farina—a kind of cream of wheat I used to eat as a kid. I have to admit that the first time I saw grits, I wasn't expecting a peak dining experience. But now I've gotten into the spirit of things, and I like grits with butter or with red-eye gravy.

Collard greens are another food that's strictly Southern. They look sorta funny, sorta like they'd been the victim of a slime attack, but they taste good. As a Yankee, what I had to tell myself was to try anything once.

And once is about all I recommend for chitterlings. I know country folk rave about them and that Raleigh's even got a Chitterling Club composed of all kinds of important people who profess to enjoy the dish.

I guess my tastebuds just aren't developed enough. Probably you have to go into training for several years, gradually eating a bit more chitterling every week or so, before you can stomach a whole meal of them.

So far, I haven't been that hungry.

The recipes here are a smattering of the kind of food Southern moms make. It's sometimes hard to write down those kinds of recipes. Most cooks seem to grow up watching their mothers create these dishes and just gradually absorb the way to do it.

Making the crust for a cobbler, for instance, is kinda like swishing a shot from back-court at the buzzer. Somebody can tell you how to do it, but it takes talent as well as directions.

But we've consulted some mighty good cooks who have done their best to share their secrets.

So even if you don't have a mansion with columns or a hoop skirt or a few acres of good earth, these dishes will give you a mighty fine taste of the South.

AVOCADO DUNK

2 very ripe avocados
½ cup mayonnaise
3 tablespoons lemon juice
1 teaspoon chili powder
1 clove garlic, finely chopped
¼ teaspoon Tabasco sauce
¼ teaspoon salt

Mash avocado or blend until smooth. Add remaining ingredients; stir well. Chill. Makes 1½ cups dip.

Serve with raw vegetables, shrimp or pineapple spears.

From Peggy Rogers, Shalimar, Fla.

CHEESE PUFFS

½ cup water
¼ cup butter
½ cup all-purpose flour
2 eggs
1/3 cup Parmesan cheese, grated
¼ cup ham, dried beef or prosciutto, finely chopped

Heat water and butter to rolling boil in saucepan. Stir flour in all at once. Stir vigorously over low heat 1 minute, until mixture leaves sides of pan and forms a ball.

Remove from heat, add eggs 1 at a time, beating well. Add cheese and ham, blend well.

Drop from teaspoon onto ungreased baking sheet. Bake in preheated 400-degree oven 18-20 minutes. Serve hot.

From Lydia George, Raleigh, N.C.

PEPPER JELLY

¾ cup green bell peppers
¼ cup hot green peppers
6 cups sugar
1½ cups cider vinegar
Green food coloring
1 (6-ounce) bottle liquid
fruit pectin

Grind peppers in blender. Use rubber gloves and do not touch face or eyes with fingers that have touched hot peppers. Bring peppers, sugar, vinegar to boil and cook for 1 minute. Remove from heat and let sit 1 minute. Add few drops of food coloring for brighter color. Add pectin and let sit 5 minutes.

Pour into 6 jelly jars.

Serve with cream cheese on crackers or as condiment with meat.

From Roberta W. McDowell, Conway, S.C.

SHRIMP BALL

2 (8-ounce) packages cream
cheese, softened
1 tablespoon onion, minced
2 tablespoons ketchup
1 tablespoon Worcestershire
sauce
½ teaspoon ground red pepper
½ teaspoon black pepper
½ teaspoon Tabasco
½ teaspoon salt
2 (8-ounce) packages frozen
or canned shrimp
Parsley, chopped
Basil, crushed

Thaw and drain shrimp. Reserve a few shrimp to garnish ball.

Mix all ingredients together forming a ball. Garnish with shrimp and chopped parsley or basil, if desired.

From Kay Warren, Raleigh, N.C.

SOUPS

AVGOLEMONO SOUP

6 cups chicken broth
1/3 cup rice, uncooked, or orzo
3 eggs
Juice of 1 lemon

Bring broth to boil. Add rice. Simmer, partially covered, for 20 minutes.

Beat eggs until frothy. Slowly add lemon juice to eggs, beating constantly. In small amounts, gradually add 1 cup of broth to lemon/egg mixture, beating constantly.

Remove soup pot from heat. Add lemon/egg mixture to hot soup, stirring gently to combine. Serve immediately.

From Mrs. John (Floye) Dombalis of the Mecca Restaurant, Raleigh, N.C. Mrs. Dombalis says this is a recipe for the traditional Greek chicken soup.

BRUNSWICK STEW

MAKES SEVEN QUARTS

1 (4-pound) chicken
½ pound pork
½ pound chuck roast
1 quart white potatoes, peeled and cubed
1 quart tomatoes
1 pint onions, chopped
3 cups lima beans
2 cups corn kernels
1 red pepper pod
2 tablespoons Worcestershire sauce
Salt
Pepper

Cook chicken, pork and beef in water to cover until tender. Cool, then cube meat. Reserve broth.

Add potatoes, onions, beans, tomatoes and seasonings to broth and cook 1 hour. Add corn, chicken, pork and beef and continue to cook until thick, stirring frequently.

From Alease Barbee, Winston-Salem, N.C.

104

MACARONI & CHEESE BAKE

SERVES EIGHT PEOPLE

1 box macaroni/cheese mix
3 cups milk
3 eggs
Cheddar cheese, grated
2 tablespoons margarine
Paprika

Cook macaroni as directed on box; spread in prepared casserole.

Beat milk and eggs together well. Pour over macaroni/cheese mix.

Dot cheese and margarine on top.

Bake in preheated 325-degree oven 50 minutes. Sprinkle with paprika.

From Susan Wester, Lillington, N.C.

RICE-CHEESE CASSEROLE

SERVES EIGHT PEOPLE

1 cup rice, cooked
1 large can evaporated milk
½ cup cooking oil
½ pound sharp cheese, grated
2 tablespoons parsley
2 eggs, beaten
1 small onion, chopped
Salt

Cook rice. Mix all ingredients together and put into greased casserole. Bake in preheated 275-degree oven 50-60 minutes.

From Carolyn Cremins of Atlanta, Ga. (Carolyn is the wife of Georgia Tech basketball coach Bobby Cremins.)

TOMATO SAUCE

2 large onions, diced
2 cloves garlic, minced
½ cup olive oil
12 large ripe tomatoes, peeled,
cored and cut up
1 cup dry red wine
½ cup water
1 bouillon cube
4 leaves basil, crushed
2 bay leaves
2 teaspoons salt
1 teaspoon sugar
1 (12-ounce) can tomato paste

Sauté onion and garlic in oil in large kettle or saucepan; stir in tomatoes and cook 5 minutes. Stir in wine and water, tomato paste, bouillon cube, basil, bay leaves, salt and sugar.

Simmer, stirring occasionally, for 1 hour or until sauce thickens. Cool. Spoon into freezer containers of desired recipe proportions. Leave ½-inch headroom. Seal, label, date and freeze.

From Molly Safrit, Raleigh, N.C.

BAKED BREADED FILET OF FLOUNDER

Flounder filets
Butter, softened
Onion salt
Bread crumbs, toasted
Parsley flakes
Paprika

Place desired number filets skin-side down in baking dish that has been greased and sprinkled with onion salt. Spread butter on fish. Sprinkle fish with bread crumbs, onion salt, parsley and paprika.

Bake in preheated 400-degree oven 12 minutes. Broil fish prepared in same way for 5 minutes.

From Annie Laurie Pomeranz, Raleigh, N.C.

BOILED HAM

1 picnic ham or shoulder
1 cup sugar
½ cup cider vinegar
3-4 tablespoons mixed pickling spices

Immerse ham in water in large pot. Add sugar, vinegar and spices. Simmer until tender. Cool and slice.

From Nancy Whiting, Elkin, N.C.

CHAFING DISH SHRIMP

2 pounds shrimp, shelled and deveined
6 tablespoons butter
3 tablespoons olive oil
6 green onions, white part only, chopped
2 small garlic cloves, minced
6 tablespoons parsley, chopped
Salt and pepper
Juice of 2 lemons
1/3 cup Pernod
1/3 cup cognac

Prepare rice and set aside. Warm cognac and Pernod prior to flambéing.

In chafing dish or pan on stove, heat oil and butter over medium heat. Add onion, garlic, shrimp and lemon juice. Using a wooden spoon, toss and cook until shrimp are heated through. Sprinkle with salt and pepper.

Warm Pernod and cognac, and flambé in pan. When flame disappears, sprinkle with parsley. Serve over rice.

From Bill Kaufman, Greensboro, N.C.

CHICKEN CASSEROLE

1 whole chicken, cooked, boned and cut into pieces
1 box wild and long grain rice, cooked as directed
1 can cream of celery soup
1 onion, chopped
1 cup mayonnaise
1 can water chestnuts, sliced
¼ cup chicken broth
1 can mushrooms, drained

Mix celery soup, mayonnaise and chicken broth thoroughly. Combine with other ingredients. Pour into greased casserole.

Bake covered, in preheated 350-degree oven 30 minutes. Remove cover and bake 15 minutes.

From Jean Durham, Chapel Hill, N.C. (Jean is the wife of sportscaster Woody Durham.)

CHICKEN GRAVY

1 cup pan drippings from
frying chicken
¼ cup flour
½-1 cup water
Salt
Pepper

Stir flour in hot drippings until brown. Lower heat; add water and blend well to creamy consistency. Add salt and pepper to taste.

From Mrs. H. A. Turlington, Sr., Dunn, N.C.

CHICKEN IN A POT

1 whole chicken
1 pinch parsley
1 small onion, chopped
3 stalks celery, sliced
3 carrots, sliced
Salt
Pepper
1 cup uncooked rice

Cover chicken with water. Bring to boil and simmer for 2 hours. Remove chicken from bones.

Boil rice in liquid in pot for 15 minutes. Place chunks of chicken meat back in pot along with rest of ingredients. Continue cooking. When vegetables are done, serve from pot with biscuits or dumplings.

From Joyce and Lefty Driesell, College Park, Md. (Joyce says this is one of Lefty's favorite dishes. Lefty, of course, is my counterpart at the University of Maryland.)

CHICKEN WITH MUENSTER CHEESE

2 whole chicken breasts, boned
and skinned
2 eggs, beaten
Fine bread crumbs, toasted, or
canned bread crumbs
4 slices Muenster cheese
½ pound fresh mushrooms or
1 (8-ounce) can mushrooms,
drained
1 cup chicken broth (or dissolve
one chicken bouillon cube in
1 cup hot water)

Cut breasts in half; remove white fibrous membrane and flatten by pounding between 2 pieces of waxed paper until very thin, being careful not to tear the meat.

Marinate chicken and egg in covered dish, several hours or overnight. When ready to cook, dip each breast into crumbs, then sauté in butter until brown on both sides. Place in baking dish in single layer.

Top each breast with cheese slice. Add enough broth to cover bottom of dish, adding more as needed during baking.

Cover with foil; bake 45-60 minutes in 350-degree oven.

From Mrs. John (Floye) Dombalis of the Mecca Restaurant, Raleigh, N.C.

CHUCK ROAST

1 (4-pound) chuck roast
3 tablespoons butter
2 tablespoons oil
Salt and pepper to taste
Garlic salt
1 package onion soup mix
1 (6-ounce) can tomato paste
1 cup water

Brown roast in butter and oil, being sure to brown on all sides. Add salt, pepper and garlic salt to taste. Add soup mix, tomato paste and water. Simmer, covered, 2-2½ hours until done.

From Carrie Lowe, Alexandria, Va. (Carrie is the mother of former N.C. State point guard Sidney Lowe, one of three sterling seniors who led us to the national championship in 1983.)

CONNIE'S CHILI

¼ cup salad oil
1 cup onion, chopped
1 cup green pepper, chopped
2 cloves garlic, crushed
2 pounds ground beef
2 (1-pound) cans tomatoes, undrained
1 (6-ounce) can tomato paste
3 tablespoons chili powder
1 tablespoon sugar
1 tablespoon salt
¼ teaspoon pepper
⅛ teaspoon paprika
2 bay leaves
1 teaspoon cumin
1 teaspoon basil leaves
6 squirts hot sauce
Dash cayenne
1 pound kidney beans
1 cup cheddar cheese, grated

Soak kidney beans overnight and cook 1½ - 2 hours.

Sauté onion, green pepper, garlic in oil. Drain. Brown beef. Drain fat.

Add all other ingredients except beans and cheese. Simmer 1 hour or until thick.

Add beans and heat gently. Serve with cheese.

From Connie Ballard, Houston, Texas.

CORN & OYSTER CASSEROLE

1½ cups cracker crumbs
1½ cups corn kernels
1 can frozen oyster stew or fresh oysters
Salt
Pepper
Bread crumbs

Place corn, oysters and cracker crumbs in layers in greased casserole until dish is full. Salt and pepper to taste. Cover top with buttered bread crumbs.

Bake in preheated 350-degree oven until brown and bubbly.

From my neighbor, Betty Artman, Cary, N.C.

COUNTRY-STYLE STEAK

1 pound round steak, beaten
to tenderize
Salt
Pepper
Butter or oil
Flour
1 cup milk or water

Salt and pepper tenderized steak. Melt butter in electric skillet; add steak and brown quickly on both sides. Push to side of pan.

Keep drippings in pan and add 2 tablespoons flour; stir to brown. Stir in milk or water, blending well. Lower heat to 325 degrees, cover and simmer for 45 minutes.

From Alease Barbee, Winston-Salem, N.C.

FRIED CHICKEN

2 cups corn oil
1 whole fryer, cut in pieces
2 cups flour
Salt
Pepper
Paprika

Rinse chicken in cold water. Sprinkle with salt, if desired. Shake chicken pieces in flour in bag to coat. Put chicken in hot oil in electric skillet; sprinkle with paprika. Cover with lid, with lid vent open. Cook until brown. Turn on other side, and brown, with lid on.

When brown on both sides, remove and drain.

From Mrs. H. A. Turlington, Sr., Dunn, N.C.

FRIED CHICKEN

1 frying chicken, cut up
Salt
Flour
Pepper
Oil

Remove skin from chicken pieces. Place pieces in lightly salted water several hours or overnight.

Half an hour before cooking, coat pieces with flour seasoned with pepper. This seals surface.

Heat oil in cast iron frying pan. Place pieces in oil, brown on both sides. Drain.

Soaking chicken pieces in salted water takes remaining blood out of veins so that when cut, cooked pieces do not "bleed."

From Chloe Puryear, Spring Lake, N.C.

HOT BARBECUE SAUCE

½ cup onion, chopped
1 (6-ounce) can tomato paste
1 clove garlic, crushed
1 tablespoon tart pickle relish
1 tablespoon sugar
1 teaspoon salt
½ teaspoon Tabasco sauce
1 tablespoon chili powder
¼ cup vinegar or lemon juice
1 cup water

Bring all ingredients to boil; continue to boil 15 minutes. Excellent for chicken and pork chops, as well as beef ribs.

From F. Roger Whitley, Jr., Hope Mills, N.C.

OVEN BEEF STEW

1 pound stew beef
1 medium onion
2 carrots
3 medium potatoes
1 (15-ounce) package mixed
frozen vegetables
1 (15-ounce) can tomatoes
1 tablespoon tapioca

Mix first 6 ingredients in casserole and sprinkle tapioca over top. Bake in pre-heated 300-degree oven for at least 3 hours or longer if desired. Stir before serving.

From Judy Graybeal, Cary, N.C. (Judy is secretary to my business manager, Dick Stewart.)

OYSTER PIE

SERVES EIGHT PEOPLE

1 pint oysters
4 cups buttered bread and
cracker crumbs
¼ pound margarine
2 cups milk
1 egg
½ teaspoon salt
Red pepper to taste

Spread layer of crumbs in buttered casserole. Put oysters on top. Add another layer of crumbs. (**Note:** Mixed bread and cracker crumbs make for a lighter pie than all cracker crumbs.)

Melt margarine. Add to milk. Beat in egg. Add salt and pepper. Pour over oysters. More milk can be added if needed. Bake at 400 degrees for 30 minutes or until brown.

From Roberta W. McDowell, Conway, S.C.

PIG PICKING SAUCE

2 quarts vinegar
½ pound butter
1 ounce black pepper
1½ ounces crushed red pepper
1½ teaspoons salt

Heat all ingredients together. Use to baste pig as it cooks. Chop or slice meat, pour sauce over meat before serving.

From Marcia Williams, Raleigh, N.C.

PORK RIBS

2 sheets pork ribs
Barbecue sauce

Rinse ribs in water. Bake in preheated 325-degree oven 60 minutes. After 30 minutes, turn ribs, baste and continue to baste until done.

From Alease Barbee, Winston-Salem, N.C.

ROAST LEG OF LAMB

½ cup ketchup
½ cup vinegar
½ cup water
Garlic salt
Leg of lamb

Mix ketchup, vinegar and water; pour enough into shallow roasting pan to cover bottom. Place leg of lamb in pan. Stick lamb several times with point of sharp knife. Sprinkle with garlic salt; cover with remaining ketchup mixture.

Stick meat thermometer in thickest part of leg. Bake in preheated 350-degree oven until thermometer indicates lamb is done. When mixture dries in bottom of pan, add 2 cups water and baste. Continue to baste and add water as needed until done.

From Annie Laurie Pomeranz, Raleigh, N.C.

SAUSALITO SCAMPI

3 whole chicken breasts
1 pound fresh or frozen shrimp
1/3 cup butter
1/3 cup oil (olive or vegetable)
2 cloves garlic, minced
1 teaspoon salt
Freshly ground pepper
Juice of 1 lemon
Parsley, chopped

Remove chicken meat from bones; cut into 1-inch pieces. Shell and devein shrimp. Heat butter and oil in large metal skillet. Add garlic and sauté for 2 minutes.

Add chicken and cook, stirring constantly, until brown. Push to side. Add shrimp and cook, stirring constantly until shrimp turns pink. Season with salt and pepper; sprinkle with lemon juice and top with parsley. Cook 1 minute longer. Serve with a dry red wine.

From Linda Foster, Coral Cables, Fla. (Linda is the wife of former Clemson University basketball coach Bill Foster, who is now at the University of Miami.)

SHISH KEBAB

2 - 2½ pounds lean lamb, cubed
in 1-inch pieces
Green peppers, 1-inch cubes
Cherry tomatoes or
tomato wedges
Small white onions, whole or
halved, and parboiled
Whole mushroom caps, fresh
or canned

In afternoon, pour marinade over cubes of lamb. Refrigerate and turn occasionally.

Skewer meat alternately with vegetables. Allow 3 - 4 cubes of meat per person. Place in broiler about 4 inches from flame. Broil 3 - 4 minutes on each side. Broil longer if well-done is preferred.

LEMON MARINADE

½ cup oil
¼ cup lemon juice
1 teaspoon salt
1 teaspoon marjoram
½ teaspoon thyme
½ teaspoon pepper
1 large garlic clove, pressed
½ cup parsley, chopped, or
2 tablespoons parsley flakes

Combine all ingredients, stir and pour over shish kebab.

From Florence Barakat, Greensboro, N.C. (Not only is Florence a great cook, but she can beat me at golf.)

SCALLOPS IN CHEESE SAUCE

Scallops
1 small carton whipping cream
Half and half
Rosemary
Tarragon
Salt and pepper
Mushrooms, sliced
½ medium onion, chopped
1½ cups white cheese, grated
Cornstarch
Butter

Sauté fresh scallops in butter. Sprinkle lightly with rosemary, tarragon, salt and pepper, and stir. Do not overcook. Place in buttered casserole dish. Add whipping cream and enough half and half to cover scallops.

Sauté mushrooms and onion in butter and stir into scallops.

Place casserole in preheated 300-degree oven. After 5 minutes stir in ½ cup cheese. Add cheese 2 more times at 5-minute intervals. Thicken with cornstarch. Test with fork for doneness. Time depends on size of scallops. Serve over rice.

From Jo Mertz, St. Petersburg, Fla.

SHRIMP CREOLE

SERVES SIX PEOPLE

1½ pounds shrimp, fresh or frozen
¼ cup onion, chopped
¼ cup green pepper, chopped
6 stalks celery, chopped
1 clove garlic, minced
¼ cup butter or other fat, melted
Dash pepper
3 tablespoons flour
1 teaspoon salt
1 (#303) can tomatoes
1 (10½-ounce) can tomato soup
1 tablespoon Worcestershire sauce
1 teaspoon Tabasco sauce
Cooked rice

Cook, clean, and devein shrimp.

Cook celery, pepper, onion and garlic in shortening until tender. Add all other ingredients except shrimp; simmer 45 minutes.

Add shrimp; simmer 15 minutes longer. Serve hot over hot cooked rice.

From Libby Frederick, Garner, N.C. (Libby is one of the secretaries in NCSU Athletic Director Willis Casey's office.)

STIR FRY DINNER FOR FOUR

Oriental Rice
4 chicken pieces, boned and cut
in bite-size pieces
4 tablespoons butter
1 cup onion, chopped
½ cup green pepper, chopped
1 cup mushrooms, sliced
½ cup celery, chopped
1 cup fresh bean sprouts
Ground ginger
Paprika
Garlic salt
Soy sauce

Sprinkle chicken with ginger, garlic and paprika.

Sauté onion and green pepper in large frying pan in 2 tablespoons butter until soft but not browned.

With heat on high, add chicken; stir quickly (use a long-handled wooden spoon) until it is well browned on all sides. Turn heat down slightly, add additional 2 tablespoons butter, celery, mushrooms and bean sprouts. Stir well to blend. Sprinkle on soy sauce, cover; let simmer about 2 minutes. Serve over rice.

ORIENTAL RICE

1 cup rice, uncooked
2 tablespoons butter
¼ cup onion, chopped
⅛ cup green pepper, chopped
1½ cups water
1 chicken bouillon cube
Ginger
Paprika
Saffron

Sauté onion and green pepper in butter in medium saucepan until soft and lightly browned. Add dash of ginger and paprika. Stir in saffron.

Add rice and stir until well coated with spices. Add water and bouillon cube. Stir well to blend. Bring to boil, reduce heat to low, cover tightly and simmer 20 minutes or until all water is absorbed. Remove cover and fluff.

From Suzanne Pomeranz, Sanford, N.C.

VEGETABLES

BEAN POT

4 tablespoons bacon drippings
2 cloves garlic, finely chopped
3 medium onions,
finely chopped
1 (16-ounce) can pork
and beans
1 (16-ounce) can kidney beans
1 small can lima beans, drained
½ cup brown sugar
¼ cup vinegar
½ cup ketchup
1 teaspoon mustard
1 teaspoon salt
½ teaspoon black pepper

Sauté onion and garlic in bacon drippings. Mix with other ingredients.

Pour into 2-quart baking dish. Bake in preheated 350-degree oven 45-60 minutes.

From Lydia George, Cary, N.C.

BLACK-EYED PEAS

1 cup freshly hulled peas
1 teaspoon sugar
¼ teaspoon salt
Water
Bacon fat

Bring peas to boil in water to cover and simmer until done.

Add bacon fat, sugar and salt. Mash a few peas against side of pan and stir well. Simmer 10 minutes to blend seasonings.

From my secretary, Frances Lewis, Cary, N.C.

BUTTERNUT SQUASH SOUFFLÉ

2 cups butternut squash,
cooked and mashed
½ teaspoon salt
¼ cup maple-flavor syrup
2 tablespoons brown sugar
3 tablespoons cornstarch
3 eggs, separated
1¼ cups evaporated milk
½ cup margarine, melted
Almonds, sliced

Combine squash, salt, syrup, sugar, cornstarch and beat until fluffy. Add egg yolks, milk and margarine, mixing well. Beat egg whites until stiff. Fold into mixture. Pour into casserole dish. Top with almonds.

Bake in preheated 350-degree oven 60 minutes.

From Mary Howard, Raleigh, N.C.

CORN PUDDING

1 can cream-style corn
1 tablespoon flour
½ cup milk
1 tablespoon sugar
1 egg
½ teaspoon baking powder
3 tablespoons margarine

Mix all ingredients together. Bake in preheated 375-degree oven 35 minutes or until firm.

From Kathy Short, Raleigh, N.C.

SQUASH PIE

1½-2 cups yellow squash,
cooked and mashed
½ cup milk
4 eggs, beaten
½-¾ cup sugar
½ teaspoon cinnamon
½ teaspoon nutmeg
¼ teaspoon ginger
¼ teaspoon allspice
¼ teaspoon cloves
1 uncooked pie crust

Combine all ingredients; pour into pie shell. Bake in preheated 375-degree oven 45 minutes.

From Clarice Jessup, Siler City, N.C.

STUFFED ZUCCHINI

Whole zucchini
Onion, chopped
Cheddar cheese, grated
Bread crumbs
Salt and pepper

Wash and then parboil number of zucchini desired for serving guests. Cool them in cold water.

Slice zucchini in half. Scoop out centers. Mix centers with onion, cheese, bread crumbs and salt and pepper. Place mixture in zucchini shells. Sprinkle with cheese.

Bake in preheated 325-degree oven 20-30 minutes until bubbly and golden brown.

From Jo Mertz, St. Petersburg, Fla.

SWEET POTATO PUDDING

2 cups sweet potatoes, cooked,
peeled and mashed
1 cup milk
1½ cups sugar
2 eggs
¾ stick margarine
½ teaspoon nutmeg
½ teaspoon cinnamon

Combine all ingredients, mixing well. Pour into casserole.

Bake in preheated 400-degree oven 20 minutes.

From Frances Lewis, Cary, N.C.

TURNIP GREENS

1 piece (6 by 2 by 1 inch)
streak-o-lean or fatback
Turnip greens

Cut halfway through fatback several times. Place in large pot with 2 inches of water. Bring to boil, reduce heat and simmer 30-45 minutes.

Wash greens well. Put salt in last rinse water to kill any insects remaining. Place greens in pot with fatback. Simmer 45 minutes, covered. Add water as needed to prevent pot from boiling dry.

To serve, remove greens with slotted spoon and place in colander. Chop greens well. Place in bowl. Skim 4 tablespoons grease from pot juices and pour over greens. Add salt to taste.

From Mae Johnson, Goldsboro, N.C.

SALADS

APRICOT SALAD

1 large can crushed pineapple,
drained (save juice)
1 large can apricots, cut fine
(save juice)
6 ounces orange-flavored
gelatin
2 cups hot water
1 cup apricot and
pineapple juice
¾ cups miniature
marshmallows
¾ cup cheese, grated

Drain fruits, reserve juice. Dissolve gelatin in hot water, add 1 cup juice and chill until slightly set. Fold in fruit and marshmallows, pour into baking dish, chill until firm. Spread with Fruit Cheese Topping. Sprinkle top with grated cheese.

FRUIT CHEESE TOPPING

½ cup sugar
3 tablespoons flour
3 tablespoons butter
1 egg, slightly beaten
1 cup pineapple-apricot juice
1 cup non-dairy whipped
topping

Combine sugar and flour. Blend in egg and juices, cook over low heat, stirring constantly, until thick. Remove from heat and add butter. Cool; fold in topping.

From Roylene Thompson, Raleigh, N.C.

BEAN SALAD

2 (15½-ounce) cans french-
style green beans, drained
1 (16-ounce) can cut green
beans, drained
1 (17-ounce) can peas, drained
¾ cup celery, minced
½ cup onion, chopped
1 medium green pepper,
finely chopped
¼ cup pimiento, chopped
1 can water chestnuts, sliced
½ cup cider vinegar
1/3 cup salad oil
1/3 cup sugar
½ teaspoon basil

Combine vegetables in bowl. Combine vinegar, sugar, oil, basil and adjust for taste. Pour over vegetables; toss to coat. Refrigerate overnight. Drain well before serving.

From Martha Paulson, Raleigh, N.C.

CAULIFLOWER SALAD

1 head lettuce, chopped
1 head cauliflower, chopped
in bite-size pieces
1 large sweet onion,
sliced thinly
1 pound bacon,
fried and crumbled
1 large can Parmesan cheese
¼ cup sugar
1 cup mayonnaise

Layer in order given in large bowl, cover tightly and refrigerate overnight. Mix about 10 minutes before serving.

From Linda Reibel, Raleigh, N.C. (Linda is the wife of Don Reibel, team doctor for the Wolfpack basketball team.)

TANGY TOMATO ASPIC

1 (6-ounce) package
lemon gelatin
2½ cups boiling water
1 (15-ounce) can tomato sauce
3 tablespoons white vinegar
1 teaspoon salt
1½ teaspoons onion juice
Dash each of Tabasco, pepper,
ground cloves and cayenne
pepper

Dissolve gelatin in water. Blend in remaining ingredients. Pour into 10 - 12 individual molds or 6-cup ring mold. Chill until firm. Serve on greens with mayonnaise.

From Florence Barakat, Greensboro, N.C.

BEST WHOLE WHEAT LOAVES

MAKES FOUR LOAVES

1 package active dry yeast
½ cup warm water
2 cups milk
4 tablespoons butter
½ cup molasses
2 teaspoons salt
2-3 cups bread flour
3 cups stone ground
whole wheat flour

Dissolve yeast in warm water in large bowl. Add milk, butter, molasses, salt and 2 cups bread flour. Mix well. Add 3 cups stone ground wheat flour and enough of remaining flour to form stiff (but sticky) dough.

Turn out on floured board and knead 8-10 minutes, until smooth and elastic. Place in a well-greased bowl, turning to grease top. Cover with plastic wrap or towel. Let rise in a warm place until double (about 1 hour).

Divide dough into quarters, shape each into a smooth ball and place on a greased baking sheet, pressing lightly to flatten bottom. Cover; let rise until double.

Bake in preheated 425-degree oven for 10 minutes. Turn heat back to 350 degrees and bake 20 minutes longer or until loaves sound hollow when tapped.

From Pat Pittman, Raleigh, N.C.

BOILED DUMPLINGS

1½ cups flour, sifted
2 teaspoons baking powder
¾ teaspoon salt
¾ cup milk

Mix all ingredients together. Drop by spoonfuls onto chicken or meat in boiling meat stock. Do not drop into liquid.

Cook 10 minutes uncovered and 10 minutes tightly covered. Remove dumplings and meat and serve. Make gravy with liquid in pan.

From Betty Artman, Cary, N.C.

BUTTERMILK BISCUITS

MAKES ABOUT 15

3 cups flour, sifted
1 tablespoon baking powder
1 teaspoon sea salt
⅛ teaspoon baking soda
½ cup butter
1 cup plus 2 tablespoons buttermilk
Additional flour
1 egg white, beaten lightly

Sift together flour, baking powder, salt and soda. Cut in butter until mixture resembles coarse cornmeal. Add buttermilk, stirring with fork to blend the ingredients.

Place dough on floured surface and knead gently for about 20-30 seconds. Roll out to ¾ inch thick. Cut with 2-inch biscuit cutter dipped in flour. (Use glass if you don't have a cutter.)

Place biscuits on lightly buttered cookie sheet and brush with egg white.

Bake in preheated 375-degree oven for 15-18 minutes.

From Roylene Thompson, Raleigh, N.C.

CORN BREAD

1 cup cornmeal
1 teaspoon onion salt
¾ cup buttermilk or water
3 tablespoons oil
Margarine

Combine meal, salt and buttermilk to make batter. Heat oil in cast-iron frying pan until hot. Pour in batter.

Bake in preheated 400-degree oven 30 minutes. Spread margarine on top and continue baking until brown.

From Mrs. H. A. Turlington, Sr., Dunn, N.C.

CORN BREAD PATTIES

White cornmeal
Water
Salt

Combine cornmeal and water to reach paste-like consistency. Salt to taste.

Scoop up enough of mixture to pat out a patty in palm of the hand.

Fry in hot oil on both sides. Drain. Serve warm with butter.

From Ann Puryear, Raleigh, N.C.

HUSH PUPPIES

10 quarts plain flour
5 pounds self-rising white cornmeal
1 quart vegetable oil
2 quarts sugar
1½ quarts onion, very finely chopped
21 eggs
1 quart buttermilk
2 quarts milk
2 quarts chicken stock
½ cup baking powder

Mix all ingredients well. Drop by spoonfuls in deep oil heated to 350 degrees. Brown well. Drain.

From David Brittain, Sea Captain's House Restaurant, Myrtle Beach and Murrell's Inlet, S.C.

HUSH PUPPIES

SERVES FOUR PEOPLE

5 cups flour
1½ cups self-rising white cornmeal
½ cup vegetable oil
1 cup sugar
¼ cup onion, chopped
2 eggs
½ cup buttermilk
1 cup milk
½ cup chicken stock
1 tablespoon baking powder

Mix all ingredients well. Drop by spoonfuls in deep oil heated to 350 degrees. Brown well. Drain.

This recipe is taken from the Sea Captain's House recipe, reduced for your convenience.

From Roberta W. McDowell, Conway, S.C.

OATMEAL BREAD

3 cups rolled quick-cooking oats
3 cups boiling water
½ cup wheat germ
1 tablespoon salt
2 tablespoons oil
½ cup honey or molasses
2 packages dry yeast
½ cup warm water
5-5½ cups whole wheat flour

Combine oats, boiling water, wheat germ, salt, oil and honey, and cool.

Mix together yeast and warm water. Blend 2 mixtures together. Add most of flour, knead, then let rise until double. Punch down. Shape into round loaf, let rise until double.

Bake in preheated 350-degree oven 50-60 minutes.

From Laura Cando, Raleigh, N.C.

ROLLS

1 cup milk, scalded
½ cup shortening
½ cup sugar
1 teaspoon salt
2 cakes fresh yeast
2 eggs, beaten
4½ cups flour
Butter, melted

Combine milk, shortening, sugar and salt. Cool to lukewarm. Add yeast and eggs. Add flour; mix to soft dough. Knead on lightly floured surface until smooth and elastic. Cover bowl and let rise in warm place until double in bulk.

Beat down. Shape balls of dough into size of golf ball. Roll each in melted butter; place in well-greased baking pan, let rise until double in bulk.

Bake in preheated 350-degree oven 30-40 minutes.

From Ellen Woodson, Middlesboro, Ky.

ORANGE MUFFINS

1 orange
1/3 cup fresh orange juice
½ stick unsalted butter, softened
1 large egg
½ cup raisins
1½ cups all-purpose flour
¾ cup sugar
1 teaspoon double acting baking powder
1 teaspoon soda
1 teaspoon salt

Grate rind from orange, reserving it; quarter and seed orange. In blender, blend reserved orange rind, orange quarters, orange juice, butter and egg. Add raisins, blend mixture 5 seconds and transfer to bowl.

Into bowl, sift flour, sugar, baking powder, soda and salt. Stir mixture into orange mixture, and stir batter until just combined.

Pour into buttered and floured muffin tins.

Bake in preheated 400-degree oven 15 - 20 minutes, until golden brown.

From Edna H. Bradshaw, Cary, N.C. (Edna is our children's baby sitter. They call her "Mrs. B.")

SQUASH FRITTERS

1 cup squash, cooked
2 tablespoons butter
Salt
Pepper
Pinch onion salt
½ cup milk
½ cup flour
½ teaspoon baking powder
1 egg
1 teaspoon sugar

Melt butter, add all other ingredients, mixing well.

Drop by spoonfuls into hot grease. Cook, turning until brown all over. Drain.

From Betty Artman, Cary, N.C.

CHAMPAGNE PUNCH

SERVES EIGHT PEOPLE

1 bottle champagne
2 quarts chablis blanc
12 ounces frozen lemonade
concentrate
Crushed ice

Mix all ingredients together and chill well before serving.

From Martha Paulson, Raleigh, N.C.

HOT SPICED CIDER

1½ gallons apple cider
3 sticks cinnamon
1 tablespoon whole cloves
1 tablespoon whole allspice
1 teaspoon anise seeds
½ teaspoon whole
cardamon seeds
½ teaspoon mint leaves
Honey, if desired

Combine all ingredients and simmer 20 minutes. To serve, pour ½-1 jigger brandy into mug. Fill with hot cider. Best if prepared 1 day in advance and reheated.

From Martha Paulson, Raleigh, N.C.

RUSSIAN TEA

1½ cups sugar
2 cups Tang
¾ cup instant tea with lemon
1 (6-ounce) box orange /
pineapple gelatin
1 teaspoon cinnamon
1 teaspoon cloves
1 teaspoon ground allspice

Combine all ingredients. Store in airtight container. To serve, add 3 teaspoons mixture to 1 cup hot water.

From Helen Upchurch, Raleigh, N.C.

SYLLABUB

Whipping cream
Powdered sugar
Blackberry wine

Whip cream until stiff. Sweeten to taste with powdered sugar. Flavor to taste with wine. Serve in cup with a spoon.

From Blanche T. French, Raleigh, N.C.

BANANAS FOSTER

SERVES ONE

2 tablespoons brown sugar
1 tablespoon butter
1 banana, peeled and
sliced lengthwise
Dash cinnamon
½ ounce banana liqueur
1 ounce white rum
Vanilla ice cream
(we use Haagen Daz)

Melt sugar and butter over medium flame. When both butter and sugar have melted together into syrupy consistency, add bananas and sauté until tender. Sprinkle with cinnamon. Pour in banana liqueur and rum and flambé. Baste bananas until flame burns out. Serve immediately over ice cream.

From Chef Debbie Barnes of MacGregor Downs Country Club, Cary, N.C. (This is my number one favorite dessert in the whole world!)

BANANA PUDDING

4 tablespoons all-purpose flour
¼ cup lemon juice
2 tablespoons butter
¾ cup sugar
½ cup water
1 egg, beaten
Dash of salt
½ teaspoon lemon rind,
grated
1 cup whipping cream,
beaten stiff
2 dozen vanilla wafers, crushed
2 bananas, sliced

Combine flour, sugar and salt in top of double boiler; add lemon juice, water and egg. Place over boiling water and cook 10 minutes or until thick, stirring constantly.

Add butter and lemon rind; cool. Put layer of filling in bottom of bowl. Crumble few vanilla wafers over. Add layer of bananas, then layer of whipped cream. Continue to alternate layers, ending with whipped cream. Garnish with a few vanilla wafer crumbs.

From Ellen Woodson, Middlesboro, Kentucky.

BOCCONE DOLCE (Sweet Mouthful)

4 egg whites
Pinch salt
¼ teaspoon cream of tartar
1 cup sugar

Beat egg whites until stiff after adding salt and cream of tartar. Gradually beat in sugar. Beat until meringue is stiff and glossy.

Line baking sheets with waxed paper. Trace 3 circles on paper, 8 inches in diameter each. Spread meringue evenly over circles, about ¼ inch thick.

Bake in preheated 250-degree oven 20-25 minutes until pale and golden. Peel paper carefully from bottom and dry meringues on cake racks. When dry, add filling.

FILLING

6 ounces semi-sweet chocolate morsels
3 tablespoons water
3 cups whipping cream
1/3 cup sugar
1 pint fresh strawberries, sliced (reserve 4 for decoration)

Melt chocolate morsels and water over hot water. Whip cream until stiff. Gradually add sugar and beat until very stiff.

Place meringue layer on serving plate. Spread with thin coat of chocolate. Spread with whipping cream and top with layer of berries. Add second meringue layer. Spread with chocolate, cream and berries. Add third meringue. Add remaining cream. Dot with whole berries.

From Jo Mertz, St. Petersburg, Fla.

CHESS PIE

1 lemon, quartered and seeded
4 eggs
1 stick butter
2 cups sugar
1 (9-inch) pie shell, unbaked

Blend all ingredients in blender until lemon is well chopped.

Pour into pie shell.

Bake in preheated 325-degree oven 30-35 minutes.

From Blanche T. French, Raleigh, N.C.

CHOCOLATE POUND CAKE

2 sticks butter or margarine
½ cup shortening
3 cups sugar
5 eggs
3 cups plain flour
½ teaspoon baking powder
¼ teaspoon salt
½ cup cocoa
1¼ cups milk
1 teaspoon vanilla

Cream butter, shortening and sugar together until light. Add eggs 1 at a time.

Blend dry ingredients together and add, alternating with milk and vanilla. Pour batter into greased and floured tube pan.

Bake in preheated 325-degree oven 1¾-2 hours. (Check after 1½ hours.)

From Kathy Short, Raleigh, N.C.

CRANBERRY CASSEROLE

3 cups apples, unpeeled
and chopped
2 cups raw cranberries
1½ cups granulated sugar
1½ cups quick cooking oatmeal
½ cup brown sugar, packed
1/3 cup flour
1/3 cup pecans, chopped
½ cup butter, melted

Combine apples, cranberries and granulated sugar in 2-quart casserole. To form topping, combine remaining ingredients, except for butter. Spread topping over cranberries. Pour butter over topping.

Bake in preheated 350-degree oven 1 hour or until bubbly and light brown. Serve hot.

From Molly Safrit, Raleigh, N.C.

DEVIL'S FOOD CAKE

½ cup butter
2 cups sugar
3 ounces unsweetened
chocolate, melted
1 teaspoon vanilla
4 egg yolks
1 cup milk
2 2/3 cups flour
4 teaspoons baking powder
4 egg whites

Cream butter and sugar. Add chocolate, vanilla and egg yolks. Stir baking powder into flour. Add flour to egg mixture alternately with milk, beating well. Beat egg whites until stiff and fold into batter. Pour into 9-by-13-by-2-inch prepared pan.

Bake in preheated 350-degree oven 45 minutes.

From Lizzie Mae Cleland, Frankfort, Ky.

EASY PEACH COBBLER

1 cup self-rising flour
1 cup sugar
1/3 cup oil
1 egg
Peaches, peeled and sliced

Place as many peaches as you want in the bottom of an 11-by-6½-inch pan.

Mix together flour, sugar, oil and egg. This will make an oily dough. Take a small piece of dough, flatten it with your hand and spread over peaches. Continue until dough has been used.

Bake in preheated 350-degree oven 40-45 minutes. Serve warm with ice cream. Blueberries are also good prepared this way.

From Mrs. William Woodward, Conway, S.C. (Vivian Woodward says do not cover or refrigerate leftover cobbler as the crust will become soggy.)

FRESH APPLE CAKE

2 cups sugar
1½ cups oil
3 eggs
3 cups all-purpose flour
1 teaspoon soda
1 teaspoon salt
1 teaspoon cinnamon
1 teaspoon vanilla
Dash ground nutmeg
3 cups apples, peeled
and chopped
1 cup nuts, broken in pieces

Mix together sugar, oil and eggs. Add remaining ingredients and mix well. Pour into greased and floured tube pan.

Bake in preheated 325-degree oven for 1¼ hours. Frost or serve with whipped cream.

ICING

1 stick margarine
2 tablespoons milk
½ cup brown sugar
½ teaspoon vanilla

Combine margarine, milk and sugar in saucepan. Bring to boil and cook at boil 1 minute. Add vanilla; beat until thick. Cool and frost cake.

From Susan Brown, Raleigh, N.C.

GRAHAM CRACKER CAKE

½ pound butter
2¼ cups sugar
5 eggs
2 teaspoons vanilla
2 teaspoons baking powder
1 cup milk
1 pound graham crackers, crushed
1 cup black walnuts or pecans
1 cup coconut, shredded
1 teaspoon cinnamon
¼ teaspoon nutmeg
¼ teaspoon cloves
1 small can crushed pineapple, drained

Cream butter and sugar. Add eggs, vanilla, baking powder and milk. Stir in graham crackers, nuts, coconut, spices and pineapple.

Butter and flour three 9-inch cake pans. Divide batter evenly among pans. Bake in preheated 350-degree oven 30 minutes. Cool completely before frosting.

ICING

¼ pound butter, softened
1 box powdered sugar
Juice from pineapple
Pinch of salt

Mix all ingredients together. Spread evenly over cake.

From Zina Barbee, Durham, N.C.

HOMEMADE ICE CREAM

3 cups milk
4-6 eggs, beaten
1-1½ cups sugar
1 can sweetened
condensed milk
1 tablespoon vanilla

Place milk in saucepan and heat until bubbling. Gradually beat in eggs. Use 4 eggs for fruit-flavored ice cream, 6 for vanilla and chocolate.

Add sugar. Use 1½ cups for fresh fruit, 1 cup for vanilla or chocolate. Beat until thick. Add condensed milk and vanilla.

Pour into ice cream freezer container and add enough milk to reach within 2½ inches from the top. Ice cream may be varied according to flavorings used.

VARIATIONS

Chocolate: Combine 8 tablespoons cocoa with sugar and milk.

Vanilla: 3 tablespoons vanilla, total.

Pineapple: 1½ cups crushed pineapple.

Fruit: 2 cups prepared fruit of your choice.

From Frances Lewis, Cary, N.C.

HUMMINGBIRD CAKE

3 cups all-purpose flour
2 cups sugar
1 teaspoon baking soda
1 teaspoon salt
1 teaspoon ground cinnamon
3 eggs, beaten
1 cup vegetable oil
1½ teaspoons vanilla extract
1 (8-ounce) can crushed
pineapple, undrained
1 cup pecans, chopped
2 cups bananas, chopped
Cream cheese frosting
½ cup pecans, chopped

Combine first 5 ingredients in large mixing bowl; add eggs and oil, stirring until dry ingredients are moistened. Do not beat. Stir in vanilla, pineapple, 1 cup pecans and bananas.

Spoon batter into 3 greased and floured 9-inch round cakepans. Bake in preheated 350-degree oven 25-30 minutes or until wooden pick inserted in center comes out clean. Cool in pans 10 minutes; remove from pans and cool completely.

Spread frosting between layers and on top and sides of cake; then sprinkle ½ cup chopped pecans on top. Yield: one 3-layer cake.

CREAM CHEESE FROSTING

1 (8-ounce) package cream
cheese, softened
½ cup butter or margarine,
softened
1 (16-ounce) package
powdered sugar, sifted
1 teaspoon vanilla extract

Combine cream cheese and butter, beating until smooth. Add powdered sugar and vanilla; beat until light and fluffy. Yield: enough frosting for one 3-layer cake.

From Edna H. Bradshaw, Cary, N.C.

LEMON SUPREME CAKE

1 box lemon supreme cake mix
½ cup sugar
¾ cup oil
1 cup apricot nectar
4 eggs

Combine cake mix, sugar, oil and nectar. Beat in eggs 1 at a time. Pour in prepared tube pan.

Bake in preheated 350-degree oven 1 hour. Check progress after 45-55 minutes. Frost. Better if prepared 1-2 days in advance. Serve with homemade vanilla ice cream.

FROSTING

1½ cups powdered sugar
⅜ cup lemon juice

Warm lemon juice. Do not boil. Mix well with powdered sugar. Punch holes in hot cake while hot and pour mixture over cake.

From Frances Lewis, Cary, N.C.

ITALIAN CHEESE DESSERT

SERVES SIX PEOPLE

1 pound Italian ricotta cheese
¼ cup confectioner's sugar
3 tablespoons liqueur
2 tablespoons instant espresso coffee
1 tablespoon unsweetened dark cocoa

Place cheese in bowl, and beat in sugar, then liqueur. Divide evenly into 6 dessert plates or sherbet cups. Chill.

Just before serving, mix instant espresso and cocoa together. Sprinkle a little of mixture lightly over each portion.

From Linnea Smith, Chapel Hill, N.C. (Linnea is the wife of University of North Carolina at Chapel Hill basketball coach Dean Smith.)

MISSISSIPPI MUD CAKE

3 sticks butter
2 cups sugar
1/3 cup cocoa
4 eggs
1 tablespoon vanilla
1½ cups self-rising flour
1½ cups pecans, chopped
1 jar marshmallow cream

Cream butter, sugar and cocoa together. Add eggs and vanilla, and mix well. Gradually add flour and nuts.

Pour into greased 9-by-13-inch pan. Bake in preheated 350-degree oven 30-40 minutes. Immediately upon removing from oven, spread marshmallow cream over cake. Let cool and ice.

ICING

1 stick butter
1 box powdered sugar
½ cup evaporated milk
1/3 cup cocoa
1 teaspoon vanilla
1 cup pecans

Cream butter; add sugar, milk, cocoa, vanilla and pecans. Ice cake.

From Linda Reibel, Raleigh, N.C.

PERSIMMON PUDDING

2 eggs
¾ cup sugar
1½ cups persimmons, sieved
1 cup milk
1 teaspoon vanilla
1 cup self-rising flour
1/3 coconut, shredded
¼ cup margarine, melted

Combine all ingredients, pour into 6-by-9-inch pan. Bake in preheated 350-degree oven 45 minutes or until done.

From Martha Paulson, Raleigh, N.C.

SOUR CREAM APPLE PIE

1 (9-inch) pie crust, uncooked
1 cup sour cream
2 tablespoons flour
¾ cup sugar
¼ teaspoon salt
1 teaspoon vanilla
1 egg
3 cups apples, diced

Combine sour cream, flour, sugar, salt, vanilla and egg. Stir in apples. Mix well and pour into pie shell.

Bake in preheated 400-degree oven 25 minutes. Sprinkle with topping.

TOPPING

½ cup brown sugar
1/3 cup flour
¼ cup butter

Blend all ingredients until crumbly in texture. Sprinkle on top of pie. Bake an additional 20 minutes. Serve warm or cold.

From Florence Barakat, Greensboro, N.C.

POUND CAKE

½ pound butter
½ cup shortening
3 cups sugar
5 eggs
3 cups cake flour, sifted
1 cup milk
½ teaspoon baking powder
1 teaspoon lemon flavoring
1 teaspoon vanilla

Cream butter, shortening and sugar. Beat in eggs, one at a time. Add baking powder to flour. Add flour to egg mixture alternately with milk, mixing well. Stir in vanilla and lemon flavoring. Pour into greased and floured tube pan.

Bake in preheated 350-degree oven for 1¼ hours.

From Minnie Black, Durham, N.C.

THUMBPRINTS

2 eggs
2/3 cup butter
2/3 cup shortening
1½ cups sugar
3½ cups flour
2 teaspoons baking powder
1 teaspoon salt
1 egg white, beaten
Pecans, chopped
Cinnamon
Sugar
Confectioner's sugar
Food coloring

Beat eggs; add butter, shortening, sugar, flour, baking powder and salt. Mix well.

Roll dough into 1-inch balls. Roll each ball in egg white, equal parts cinnamon and sugar and chopped pecans. Press down in center of ball with thumb. Place on cookie sheet.

Bake in preheated 375-degree oven 8-10 minutes. Remove from oven. Cool. Fill centers with colored confectioner's sugar.

From Patti Stewart, Raleigh, N.C. (Patti is the wife of my business manager, Dick Stewart.)

WHISKEY BALLS

1 large box vanilla wafers
3 tablespoons cocoa
3 tablespoons corn syrup
½ cup granulated sugar
1 cup nuts, chopped
¼ cup bourbon
Powdered sugar

Crush vanilla wafers in blender. Add remaining ingredients except powdered sugar, mixing well. Roll into 1-inch balls. Roll each ball in powdered sugar.

From Jerry Bobbitt, Hope Mills, N.C.

TAILGATING TREATS

In the New York City area, we had the Knicks, the Nets, the Giants, the Jets, the Yankees, the Mets, the Rangers, the Cosmos, etc. Pro sports were king, and college sports were just a tiny part of the total sports picture.

In North Carolina, we have the Blue Devils, the Demon Deacons, the Pirates, the Tar Heels and the Wolfpack at the Division IA level. College sports are in the spotlight. I don't think there's a fan in this area who roots for a team for any reasons other than he or she went to the school, and loved it, or adopted it and now follows its athletic fortunes with a devotion equal to the love some of the school's graduates feel for their alma mater.

My first experience with that kind of enthusiasm — an actual *love* for your school — was when my family and I came to N.C. State and started joining the fans who tailgate at the Wolfpack's home football games. Tailgating parties are like family reunions and can be as elegant or as informal as you like. Each week you see your friends before, sometimes during and usually after the game. You share good food and relax. And the whole day becomes a festive occasion.

Whether you prepare a breakfast, lunch or dinner menu, your tailgating party is a unique way of entertaining — a feast of finger food comprised of an amazing variety of tasty dishes, everything from zesty appetizers to scrumptious desserts. People who tailgate are usually hard-core sports fans who enjoy nothing better than cheering their team on to victory. But it is also very satisfying — and very important — to them to see the young athletes on the field progress and mature in their scholastic endeavors as well as their athletic exploits.

Many veteran tailgaters come to every game, both at home and away, week after week. At home games, they may have a pig pickin' or cook chicken and pork ribs on pig cookers. Bobby Commander of Raleigh and Marek Alapin of Fuquay-Varina both have big pig pickin's every year.

Tailgaters show their true school colors. Larry and Carol Hall have an N.C. license plate on their motor home that reads "WOF-PAK." Marek Alapin travels in a red and white recreational vehicle. You can hear him coming a mile away, because he always drives up playing the N.C. State fight song full blast over his exterior loudspeakers. And when he sets up in the parking lot, he unfurls not only the North Carolina flag but the NCSU flag as well. And he also has a spiffy red and white canopy for his R.V.

People who go to college football games in North Carolina are proud to stand up for their teams — regardless of their age — and are not embarrassed to wear their red and white or their blue or their black and gold or their purple and gold. I think it's wholesome. It's the way college athletics is supposed to be.

Of course, Wolfpack football games couldn't start without Larry and Carol Hall there. The Sawreys, the Halls, the Meares, the Joneses and Will Roach are really good friends of the Wolfpack. These people really enjoy life. And that is what tailgating is all about.

CHEESE DAINTIES

MAKES 60

2 cups flour
2 sticks butter
½ pound sharp cheddar cheese, grated
½ teaspoon salt
½ teaspoon cayenne pepper
2½ cups Rice Krispies

Blend flour, butter, cheddar, salt and pepper in food processor quickly. Add Krispies by hand last. Stir. Chill in refrigerator.

Pinch into small balls and flatten by hand on ungreased cookie sheet. Bake in preheated 350-degree oven 15 minutes. Do not brown too much.

From Dot Meares, Raleigh, N.C.

GREEN PEPPER & CREAM CHEESE DIP

1 tablespoon margarine
1 tablespoon sugar
1 tablespoon vinegar
1 egg, beaten
8 ounces cream cheese, softened
½ small green pepper, diced
½ small onion, diced

Mix margarine, sugar, vinegar and egg. Cook over low heat, stirring until thick. Cool.

Add cream cheese, pepper and onion and blend well. Chill. Serve with crackers. Refrigerates well several days.

From Marie Jones, Raleigh, N.C.

RAW VEGETABLE DIP

1 cup mayonnaise
1 teaspoon celery salt
1 teaspoon dried onion flakes
1 cup sour cream
1 teaspoon parsley flakes
1 teaspoon dill weed

Mix all ingredients together several hours ahead or day before. Yields 2 cups. Serve with fresh vegetables.

From Marie Jones, Raleigh, N.C.

SALMON BALL

1 (7¾-ounce) can red or pink salmon, drained and flaked
8 ounces cream cheese, softened
1 tablespoon lemon juice
2 teaspoons onion, finely minced
1 teaspoon white horseradish
¼ teaspoon salt
¼ teaspoon Liquid Smoke

Combine all ingredients. Shape into ball. Wrap well and refrigerate. Serve with crackers.

From Marie Jones, Raleigh, N.C.

SHRIMP DIP

1 (7-ounce) can shrimp,
drained and crumbled
8 ounces whipped
cream cheese
3 tablespoons onion, minced
1 tablespoon green pepper,
diced
½ cup mayonnaise
1 tablespoon ketchup

Mix all ingredients and refrigerate. Serve with crackers.

From Marie Jones, Raleigh, N.C.

SPINACH DIP

6 ounces sour cream
1 cup mayonnaise
1 (10-ounce) package frozen
chopped spinach, thawed and
drained well
1 can water chestnuts, sliced
and drained
1 package vegetable soup mix
1 small onion, chopped

Mix all ingredients. Chill overnight; serve with crackers.

From Rodney Sawrey, Smithfield, N.C.

ENTRÉES

EGG SALAD SPREAD

2 hard-boiled eggs, chopped
1 small stalk celery, chopped
¼ green pepper, chopped
1 tablespoon mayonnaise
¼ teaspoon salt
Dash pepper

Blend all ingredients. Spread on bread. For zestier flavor add 1 teaspoon sweet pickle relish to egg mixture.

From Marie Jones, Raleigh, N.C.

HAM DELIGHTS

2 sticks margarine, softened
3 tablespoons prepared mustard
3 tablespoons poppy seed
1 medium onion, grated or finely chopped
1 teaspoon Worcestershire sauce
3 packages party rolls
Swiss cheese slices
Ham slices

Split party rolls by slicing through horizontally. Blend margarine, mustard, poppy seed, onion, Worcestershire and spread on top and bottom of rolls.

Layer with cheese and ham. Cover lightly with foil.

Bake in preheated 400-degree oven 20 minutes. If rolls are not separated until after filling, and then cut apart, this process is easy. You may add turkey or chicken slices.

From Dot Meares, Raleigh, N.C.

HAMBURGER PATTIES

2 pounds ground beef
½ cup oatmeal
7 ounces ketchup
1 egg
1 green pepper, chopped
1 medium onion, chopped
Salt and pepper

Mix all ingredients. Shape into patties. Grill.

From Carol Hall, Fuquay-Varina, N.C.

ORIGINAL SANDWICH SPREAD

2 (8-ounce) packages cream cheese, softened
¼ cup mayonnaise
1 tablespoon Worcestershire sauce
1 medium onion, finely chopped
2 large green peppers, finely diced
Salt and pepper

Blend cheese, mayonnaise and Worcestershire sauce with electric mixer until creamy. Add onion, green pepper and salt and pepper to taste. Makes enough for 15 sandwiches. Cut sandwiches into wedges or strips.

From Dot Meares, Raleigh, N.C.

PORK CHOPS

Boneless pork chops
Shortening
Flour

Season and flour the number of pork chops desired for occasion. Fry slowly in melted shortening until brown. Drain.

From Larry Hall, Fuquay-Varina, N.C.

SLOPPY JOES

SERVES 16 PEOPLE

3 pounds ground beef
1 cup ketchup
1 can tomato soup
⅛ teaspoon pepper
1 medium onion, finely chopped
1 cup celery, finely chopped
1 teaspoon salt
Cheddar cheese, shredded

Brown meat. Add onion, celery, salt and pepper. Cook until tender. Drain.

Add salt and blend with ketchup and soup. Simmer 30 minutes. Serve on split hamburger buns. Top with cheddar cheese if desired.

From Norma Ausley, Holden Beach, N.C. (Norma is the wife of "The Voice of the Wolfpack," Wally Ausley.)

BAKED BEANS WITH A TWIST

1 (1-pound 12-ounce)
can beans
1/3 cup sherry
2 tablespoons brown sugar
1 teaspoon dry mustard
1 teaspoon instant
coffee powder

Mix together and bake in 350-degree oven until hot (20-30 minutes) or put into saucepan on stove and heat. Sherry and coffee add nutty flavor that is impossible to identify, but easy to enjoy.

From Carolyn Cremins, Atlanta, Ga.

MARINATED CARROTS

2 pounds carrots, peeled
and sliced
1 medium onion, peeled
and sliced thin
1 small green pepper, sliced thin
1 can tomato soup
½ cup oil
1 cup sugar
¼ cup vinegar
1 teaspoon mustard sauce
1 teaspoon Worcestershire
sauce
Salt and pepper

Boil carrots in salt water until fork tender. Do not overcook. Drain and let cool. Alternate layers of carrots, onions and pepper in bowl.

Mix all other ingredients together and pour over. Let stand in refrigerator for at least 24 hours.

From Carol Hall, Fuquay-Varina, N.C.

MARINATED CARROT STICKS

8 small carrots, cut in strips
3 tablespoons vinegar
3 tablespoons oil
1 small clove garlic
¾ teaspoon seasoned salt
¼ teaspoon salt

Heat vinegar, oil and seasonings; pour over carrot sticks. Marinate 6 hours or overnight.

From Elizabeth Sawrey, Smithfield, N.C.

COLE SLAW

2½ pounds cabbage, chopped
½ cup onion, chopped
½ cup green pepper, chopped
¼ cup pimiento, chopped
1 cup sugar
1 tablespoon salt
1 teaspoon celery seed
1 teaspoon dry mustard
½ cup vinegar
½ cup oil

Mix vegetables, sugar and salt and let stand 1 hour. Drain.

Mix celery seed, mustard, vinegar, oil. Pour over cabbage mixture, cover and refrigerate.

From Elizabeth Sawrey, Smithfield, N.C.

MARINATED MACARONI SALAD

8 ounces uncooked elbow macaroni
¾ cup Italian salad dressing
1 cup celery, chopped
¾ cup carrots, shredded
¾ cup green pepper, chopped
¼ cup onion, chopped
Sour cream

Cook macaroni by package directions until tender. Drain and rinse with cold water. Drain.

Combine macaroni and dressing. Cover and chill overnight. Before serving, toss with shredded vegetables and 2-3 tablespoons sour cream. Add salt and pepper to taste.

From Marie Jones, Raleigh, N.C.

PEA SALAD

1 can small green peas
2 cucumbers, diced
1 onion, diced
1 tomato, diced
½ cup mayonnaise
¼ cup vinegar
8 ounces cheese, grated
1 green pepper, diced
½ head lettuce, chopped

Mix mayonnaise and vinegar in bowl. Combine peas, cucumber, tomato, onion, bell pepper and lettuce. Toss pea mixture with mayonnaise mixture. Add cheese and toss. Cover and chill overnight.

From Rodney Sawrey, Smithfield, N.C.

POTATO SALAD

7 or 8 Irish potatoes
1 small onion, chopped
1 medium green pepper, chopped
3 or 4 boiled eggs, chopped
½ teaspoon mustard
3 tablespoons cubed sweet pickle
Salt and pepper to taste
Salad dressing
Paprika

Boil potatoes in jackets; cool, peel and dice. Add green pepper, onion and boiled eggs and mix well with potatoes. Add remaining ingredients; sprinkle paprika over top after mixing.

From Carol Hall, Fuquay-Varina, N.C.

RED & WHITE CONGEALED SALAD

6 ounces strawberry gelatin
1 cup boiling water
1 large can crushed pineapple, undrained
3 bananas, mashed
1 cup nuts
16 ounces strawberries
8 ounces sour cream

Dissolve gelatin in water. Add pineapple, bananas, nuts and strawberries. Pour half of mixture into dish. Chill. Spread sour cream on top. Pour remaining gelatin over sour cream. Chill until firm.

From Susan Sawrey, Raleigh, N.C.

RAW BROCCOLI SALAD

1 bunch broccoli
1 bunch green onions, sliced
4 hard-boiled eggs, coarsely
chopped
½ cup mayonnaise
¼-½ cup green olives, sliced
Salt and pepper to taste

Cut broccoli into bite-size pieces, including tender part of stem. Combine all ingredients. Refrigerate at least 2 hours.

Note: Do not use salad dressing.

From Norma Ausley, Holden Beach, N.C.

SCANDINAVIAN SALAD

1 small bunch celery, sliced
and cut fine
1 small can green peas, drained
2 medium onions, chopped
1 small can french-style
green beans, drained
1 small can pimiento, chopped
1 cup vinegar
½ cup salad oil
1 cup sugar
Salt to taste
½ teaspoon paprika
Pepper to taste

Mix last 6 ingredients and pour over vegetables that have been mixed together. Store in refrigerator. Keeps well for several days.

From Carol Hall, Fuquay-Varina, N.C.

BREADS & BEVERAGES

ANGEL BISCUITS

1 package dry yeast
2-3 tablespoons warm water
5 cups all-purpose flour
3-5 tablespoons sugar
1 tablespoon baking powder
1 teaspoon salt
1 teaspoon soda
1 cup shortening
2 cups buttermilk

Dissolve yeast in warm water. Sift dry ingredients together. Cut in shortening; stir in yeast and buttermilk. If you refrigerate part of dough, let it rise before baking.

Bake in preheated 400-degree oven 20 minutes. Serve with thin slices of ham or turkey.

From Roylene Thompson, Raleigh, N.C.

MEXICAN CORNBREAD

1 pound ground beef
½ cup onion, chopped fine
2/3 cup oil
1 pound can cream-style corn
¾ cup milk
1½ cups self-rising cornmeal
1 teaspoon salt
1-1½ cups cheddar cheese, grated
½ cup jalapeno peppers, chopped, or green chili peppers

Brown meat. Drain on paper towels. Mix together onion, salt, milk, corn and cornmeal.

Pour half of mixture in greased 10-inch cast-iron skillet. Add meat, cheese and peppers. Add remaining cornmeal mixture. Top with remaining cheese.

Bake in preheated 350-degree oven for 1 hour.

From Mabel Alapin, Fuquay-Varina, N.C. (via her sister Pat Tilley).

BEST-EVER BROWNIES

Favorite brownie recipe or
1 box family-size brownie mix
3 (8-ounce) almond
Hershey bars

Prepare brownie batter. Pour half batter in greased and floured 9-by-13-inch pan. Lay chocolate bars on batter. Pour remaining batter on top. Bake according to brownie recipe directions. Cool completely and cut into squares.

From Dot Meares, Raleigh, N.C.

CHOCOLATE FUDGE SQUARES

2 cups sugar
4 tablespoons cocoa
4 eggs
1½ cups plus 1 tablespoon flour
½ teaspoon baking powder
½ teaspoon salt
1 cup pecans, chopped
1 teaspoon vanilla
2 sticks margarine, melted

Sift sugar and cocoa. Add eggs, 1 at a time, beating well. Sift flour, salt and baking powder and add to egg mixture. Combine pecans, vanilla and margarine and add to batter. Pour into prepared pan.

Bake in preheated 350-degree oven 20 minutes or until done.

From Carol Hall, Fuquay-Varina, N.C.

CHOCOLATE FUDGE CAKE

2 cups flour
2 cups sugar
1 cup water
1 stick margarine
1 cup vegetable oil
4 tablespoons cocoa
½ cup buttermilk
2 eggs
1 teaspoon soda
Dash salt

Mix flour and sugar in large bowl.

Combine water, margarine, oil and cocoa in saucepan. Bring to boil and boil 1 minute, stirring constantly. Add to flour/sugar mixture and stir well. Add buttermilk, eggs, soda and salt. Mix well.

Pour into greased and floured 13-by-9-by-2-inch pan. Bake in preheated 350-degree oven 40 minutes. Ice in pan while cake is hot.

ICING

4 tablespoons milk
4 tablespoons cocoa
1 stick butter
1 teaspoon vanilla
1 box powdered sugar

Combine milk, cocoa, butter and vanilla and bring to boil. Sift powdered sugar and add to milk/cocoa mixture. Pour over hot cake in pan. Let cool and cut into squares.

From Carol Hall, Fuquay Varina, N.C.

CREAM CHEESE SQUARES

1 package yellow cake mix
1 egg
1 stick butter, softened
1 box powdered sugar
2 eggs
8 ounces cream cheese, softened

Combine cake mix, egg and butter. Press in greased 9-by-11 or 9-by-13-inch pan.

Mix sugar, eggs and cream cheese, blend well. Pour on top of cake mixture.

Bake in preheated 350-degree oven for 30-45 minutes. Cut into squares to serve.

From Elizabeth Sawrey, Smithfield, N.C.

HELLO DOLLY COOKIES

1 stick margarine
1 cup graham cracker crumbs
1 cup flaked coconut
16 ounces chocolate chips
1 cup pecans, chopped
1 can sweetened condensed milk

Melt margarine in rectangular baking dish. Sprinkle graham cracker crumbs evenly over margarine.

Add in layers, but do not mix, all remaining ingredients in order shown.

Be sure to drizzle milk slowly over other ingredients.

Bake in preheated 350-degree oven 25 minutes. Cool 15 minutes, cut into squares. Remove when completely cool.

From Pat George, Raleigh, N.C.

HERSHEY CHOCOLATE PIE

20 regular-size marshmallows
½ cup milk
9 Hershey Almond Bars
1 cup non-dairy whipped topping
1 cooked pie shell

In medium saucepan, combine marshmallows and milk. Cook over low heat, stirring occasionally, until marshmallows are melted.

Add Hershey bars, broken in several pieces, and continue cooking, stirring constantly, until chocolate is melted. Remove from heat. Pour into 9-by-9-by-2-inch pan. Place in freezer to cool quickly, about 10 minutes.

Fold 1 cup whipped topping into chocolate mixture. Pour into shell.

Place in freezer to chill quickly, at least 3 hours or overnight. Take from freezer to serve (pie will be soft). Add more topping around chocolate pie. Decorate top with swirls of topping.

From Linda Baum, Fayetteville, N.C.

SPICY OATMEAL COOKIES

MAKES 25-30

1½ sticks butter
½ cup sugar
1 cup brown sugar
1 egg
2 tablespoons water
1 teaspoon vanilla
2/3 cup all-purpose flour
2 teaspoons cinnamon
½ teaspoon salt
½ teaspoon baking soda
3 cups quick oats

Cream butter and both sugars. Add egg and beat well. Stir in water and vanilla.

Sift together flour, cinnamon, salt and baking soda. Add to egg mixture. Stir in oats. Drop by spoonfuls onto cookie sheets.

Bake in preheated 350-degree oven 15-17 minutes, until edges are brown but centers are soft. Remove to rack and cool.

From Susan Sawrey, Raleigh, N.C.

A DECATHLON OF FINE DINING

"On the road again . . ." Hey, Willie Nelson's concert tours are Sunday drives compared to my travel schedule for basketball and business. It seems like I spend more time in airports than a Hare Krishna.

One major fringe benefit of this travel, though, is that I get to eat at some of the finest restaurants, coast to coast. And I'm not just talking about places awarded four stars by some travel guide.

Sure, some of the swankier restaurants—the ones regularly featured in gourmet magazines—are among my favorites. But so, too, are some of those out-of-the-way places that specialize in seafood or ethnic or regional cuisine. The editors of travel guides may not know about them, but the locals sure do. Just look at their parking lots!

There's another thing, too, about eating out. I guess you'd call it the "ambience" of the restaurant. I look not only for good food, but also for a pleasant atmosphere. I like a comfortable place, a friendly place, where you can relax and feel right at home.

And that's just the way you feel when you go to Leno's Clam Bar in New Rochelle, N.Y., the fictional suburban locale of the old "Dick Van Dyke Show" and the real-life location of Iona College, where I coached right before I came to N.C. State. I used to take my family and my friends to Leno's, which is locally known as "Greasy Nick's." (In fact, everybody who works there has a shirt that says "Greasy Nick's.") And it was one of Pam's and my favorite places to take anyone who visited us.

When you get to the right part of New Rochelle, all you have to do is look for the line outside Greasy Nick's, which is located right across the street from the New York Athletic Club, a very ritzy place (especially in contrast to this outdoor restaurant where everyone— rich, middle class, poor—has to line up to take his turn at one of about 10 tables).

When it's your turn, you walk inside, grab a few beers or some soda and sit down. The waiter will write your order right on the table itself, and bring whichever of the house specialties you crave, whether it's hamburgers, hot dogs, steamers (i.e., soft-shell clams) or corn-on-the-cob soaked in butter. And everything is great!

Greasy Nick's is such a special place. If you aren't feeling too good, it's a great place to go to cure the blues. And if you have something you want to celebrate, it's a nice place to go with friends. In fact, you *gotta* go with friends to Greasy Nick's.

When I decided to devote a section of this cookbook to 10 "perfect" meals—dinners you can prepare in your own kitchen—I put Leno's Clam Bar close to the top of my list. However, the restaurant's owner, Pat Leno, turned us down. How, he wondered, can you give a "recipe" for hamburgers, hot dogs and corn-on-the-cob? The answer is, You can't. But Leno does have a dynamite recipe for fixing soft-shell clams. And this is it:

STEAMERS

2 dozen soft-shell clams
1 stalk celery
1 cup water

Rinse clams under running water. Put celery and water in pan; bring to boil. Add clams. Reduce heat and simmer 1 minute.

Remove clams to plate. Save broth for dipping. Serve clams with broth and melted butter.

This recipe makes a meal for one person or an appetizer for two people.

Even though Greasy Nick's is not numbered among the favorite restaurants represented in the decathlon of fine dining that follows, I'm sure you'll be more than satisfied with the variety of meals included. **Mangia!**

La Camelia

New York, N.Y.

DINNER FOR SIX

Gamberi, Erbe Fresche
Spaghettini con Broccoli
Costolette di Vitello Funghi Porcini
Fresh Strawberries, Balsamic Vinegar
Wine: A white wine such as Gavi

La Camelia is one of those Italian restaurants in New York with a fabulous reputation. Somebody's always writing about it. And although I do love the food and atmosphere there, La Camelia is special to me for a very personal reason.

My brother Nick and I were very, very close throughout my childhood. But, as happens in many families, when we got older we started going our separate ways and didn't see as much of each other.

About two years ago, however, I was in New York to speak at a luncheon when suddenly Nick, who works for Wang, shows up. He'd heard I was going to be there from somebody in the family.

After I'd made the talk, he said, "Come on, I want to take you out to eat and I know a place you'll really like."

So he and I and a couple more friends went over to La Camelia. We didn't even order. We just told them to keep bringing us food and wine, and we liked it all.

We ate and drank and had a great conversation. We kept talking about when we were growing up. It was what a great meal is supposed to be. You're with someone you care about, and everything is enhanced by the food and the atmosphere.

This is a fancy place, folks, but it reminded me of being a kid again at home when everyone would gather at dinner and we'd find out what everybody had been doing that day and what they were thinking about.

Since that time, I've stayed in closer touch with my brother.

Later I found out more about the restaurant. It specializes in northern Italian cuisine, which is markedly different from that of southern Italy. Seafood, bass, shrimp and sole from the Adriatic Sea play a big part on the menu. Foods aren't heavily spiced and tomatoes aren't even used as a primary ingredient. That may be hard to imagine for those who always think of Italian food in terms of something red.

Chef-owner Carlo Gaudenzi brings his own interpretation, of course, to the traditional cuisine, which is influenced by French cuisine. Like the French, northern Italians use lots of cream.

La Camelia's decor reflects its name—the chair seats have a flower design and, in season, a single blossom floats in a bowl of water on each table. Lots of bouquets are scattered throughout the dining area and the piano bar. It's kind of like a garden. Skylights even let the sun or the moon shine in.

Gaudenzi suggested this menu because it features lots of fresh vegetables and herbs and is balanced in color, flavor and texture.

Here's to you, Nick.

La Camelia, 225 East 58th Street, New York, N.Y. 10022.   Telephone: 212/751-5488.   Hours: 12 a.m.-3 p.m. Monday-Friday; 5:30 p.m.-1 a.m. Monday-Saturday. Closed Sunday and some holidays.   Credit cards: All major credit cards. Personal checks accepted.   Price range: Entrées begin at $14.   Getting there: The restaurant is between 2nd and 3rd streets, a 10-minute walk east of Rockefeller Center.

GAMBERI, ERBE FRESCHE (Shrimp, Fresh Herbs)

24 jumbo shrimp, split and deveined
6 ounces clam juice
4 garlic cloves, chopped
2 pinches thyme leaves
2 pinches fresh Italian parsley
2 pinches fresh chives
2 shallots, chopped
4 ounces butter
4 ounces olive oil
6 ounces vegetable oil
4 ounces dry white wine
2 tablespoons fresh seasoned bread crumbs

Sauté shrimp in vegetable oil. Remove.

In skillet, sauté shallots and garlic. Combine fresh herbs, white wine, butter and clam juice. Reduce one-third.

Add seasoned bread crumbs to thicken sauce. Warm shrimp in ovenproof plate. Cover with sauce and serve.

SPAGHETTINI CON BROCCOLI (Spaghettini with Broccoli)

1 pound spaghettini
Broccoli florets without stems
Medium-size tomatoes, peeled, seeded and diced
4 cloves fresh garlic, thinly sliced
4 tablespoons Parmesan cheese
5 ounces olive oil

Cook florets in salted, boiling water for few minutes. Add spaghettini. Cook 5-8 minutes. Drain.

In skillet, sauté garlic in olive oil. Add tomatoes. Cook 1-2 minutes. Mix spaghettini and florets with tomatoes. Add Parmesan and serve.

COSTOLETTE DI VITELLO FUNGHI PORCINI
(Veal Chops with Porcini Mushrooms)

6 lean veal chops with bone,
approximately 12 ounces each,
trimmed and flattened
½ pound fresh Porcini
mushrooms, thinly sliced
and washed
4 ounces butter
4 ounces olive oil
½ cup all-purpose flour
Salt and pepper
Dry white wine
2 pressed garlic cloves
Parsley

Dip veal chops in flour, shake off excess and season with salt and pepper.

Melt butter and 2 ounces oil in frying pan and, when hot, add veal and brown on both sides over medium heat. Sprinkle with wine; let simmer couple of minutes.

In meantime, in small frying pan, add 2 ounces oil with garlic. When garlic is golden brown, remove and add mushrooms. Cook quickly. Salt and pepper.

Place veal chops on hot serving platter. Place mushrooms over chops; pour on pan juices. Garnish with parsley and serve.

FRESH STRAWBERRIES, BALSAMIC VINEGAR

2 pints fresh strawberries,
washed and sliced
3 tablespoons sugar
1 tablespoon Balsamic vinegar

In salad bowl, mix 4 very ripe strawberries, sugar and balsamic vinegar until smooth. Add rest of strawberries. Mix well. Serve.

IL VAGABONDO

New York, N.Y.

DINNER FOR SIX

Special Salad
Gnocchi
Veal Parmigiana
Spinach
Bocce Ball

*Wine: A Chianti Reserva
or a Chianti Classico*

Ah. Il Vagabondo.

This is probably the only place in New York where you can still eat and then watch people play bocce—a purely Italian game that's sort of like bowling on the lawn.

Il Vagabondo brings back not only memories of watching the older generation play bocce but also of a night I'll never forget.

That was where we ate after the game the night my Iona College team upset a very fine University of Louisville team, 77-60, in Madison Square Garden. We sold out the Garden that night, and 19,000 fans saw one of the truly great college basketball games ever played in the Big Apple.

The scrappy Iona team that won it made it into the NCAA Tournament that season, and those Louisville Cardinals regrouped and won the national championship.

That first time I went to Il Vagabondo was with P.J. Carlesimo, who is now a coach at Seton Hall.

Il Vagabondo is a place with a special environment. Its co-owner and operator, David Zoni, calls his restaurant a trattoria, which is simply the Italian version of a Mom-and-Pop place. Outside, it looks rather like a hole-in-the-wall.

There are three rooms for dining and to reach them you pass through an open kitchen. If you're not hungry when you walk in, the simmering sauces will soon correct that.

We always have fun looking at the pictures of the athletes on the walls and playing Sports Trivia. What can I say. I usually win.

Gnocchi—Italian dumplings—are one of the house specialties so Zoni sent us a recipe for that.

To make the Bocce Ball in the menu above, all you have to do is serve a scoop of ice cream topped with chocolate sauce and sprinkled with nuts.

That's the part of the menu my wife assigns me.

Il Vagabondo, 351 East 62nd Street, New York, N.Y. 10021.   Telephone: 212/832-9221.   Reservations not accepted.   Hours: noon-3 a.m. Monday-Friday; 5:30 p.m.-midnight Saturday-Sunday. Closed all major holidays and three weeks in July.   Credit cards: All major credit cards. No personal checks.   Bar service. Getting there: The restaurant is located between 1st and 2nd avenues on the East Side.

SPECIAL SALAD

Ham, sliced or chopped
Salami, sliced or chopped
Cauliflower florets
String beans, blanched
and drained
Lettuce, chopped
Olive oil
Wine vinegar

Prepare enough ham, salami and vegetables to serve guests. Toss with olive oil and wine vinegar. This is an antipasto salad but not so filling.

GNOCCHI

2 pounds mealy potatoes
2½ - 3 cups flour
1 teaspoon white pepper
1¼ teaspoons salt
1 egg, slightly beaten
Bolognese sauce (meat sauce)

An hour and a half before serving, place potatoes in boiling water with 1 teaspoon salt; boil until just tender, about 15 minutes. Peel immediately and put through potato ricer or food mill, or mash.

With 2-tined fork or with hands, mix together in large bowl until blended: potatoes, 2½ cups flour, salt, white pepper and egg. On floured board knead lightly, adding more flour until dough is not sticky; firm but still soft. The best way to determine if there is enough flour is to form a little dumpling and boil it to see if it holds together.

While dough is still warm, form into ropes (¾ inch thick); cut into pieces 1 inch long. Press lightly between forefinger and thumb to make traditional gnocchi shape. Do not let gnocchi touch each other.

To cook, place a few at a time in 4 quarts boiling, salted water, cooking them in 3 batches until they rise to top; then cook 2-3 minutes longer.

Lift out with slotted spoon to cloth to drain, arranging them so they do not touch.

Place in shallow buttered baking dish; top with pats of butter if desired, Parmesan cheese and tomato and meat sauce; keep warm in 300-degree oven until served.

VEAL PARMIGIANA

6 veal cutlet slices
(about 3 pounds)
Flour
Egg, beaten
Bread crumbs
Tomato sauce
Fontina cheese, sliced

Pound veal thin with meat tenderizer. Dredge through flour, egg and then into bread crumbs. Fry breaded veal cutlet in very hot oil until golden brown. Pat excess oil off. Cover top of veal cutlet with a light tomato sauce and two slices of cheese. Pop into the broiler until the cheese melts.

Note: If you need a tomato sauce recipe, one is included in the section on the South.

SPINACH

Spinach
Juice of ½ lemon
Salt

Clean, wash and drain fresh spinach. Put small amount of water in the bottom of saucepan. Add pinch of salt and the lemon juice.

Place spinach in saucepan and bring water to boil. Simmer until spinach is soft. Remove spinach and allow it to cool. Put cooled spinach in frying pan and sauté in butter until warmed.

BOCCE BALL

Vanilla ice cream
Chocolate ice cream
Hazelnuts
Chocolate sauce
(see index for recipe)

Il Vagabondo suggests that this dinner be topped off with espresso or cappucino and a "*bocce* ball" dessert, which consists of a combination of vanilla and chocolate ice cream stuffed with a sprinkling of hazelnuts, shaped into a ball and dipped in semisweet chocolate.

Although the restaurant declined to furnish a recipe for this widely acclaimed house specialty, you can achieve similar results at home, perhaps using Ruth Stewart's chocolate sauce recipe in this book.

RYAN MCFADDEN

New York, N.Y.

DINNER FOR SIX

Vegetable Consommé
Steamed Mussels with Tomato Broth
Ryan McFadden's Stuffed Steak
Garlic Mashed Potatoes
Sautéed Butter-Glazed Carrots
Jimmy V's Grand Marnier Soufflé

*Wine: A Cabernet Sauvignon
from California's Napa Valley*

One of the three owners of Ryan McFadden is Steve McFadden—and we go a long way back.

He's an Iona College graduate and a bit of an entrepreneur. He started out as a high school teacher in New York City, then opened a restaurant out in the Hamptons in the summertime. But he always wanted a place in Manhattan.

He was one of the first believers that we could get the job done at Iona, and his dream of a great restaurant and mine of a great basketball team were growing at the same time.

We were really getting good, so we started a booster club and our first real luncheon was at Ryan McFadden, this steakhouse Steve had just opened in the city. It wasn't finished yet. We were almost sitting outside. The doors weren't even up, and people kept walking by and looking at this coach making a pep talk right out there in the wintertime.

His place came to reality and so did my basketball team. So whenever I go back to New York, I stop in at this traditional steakhouse. The restaurant is greatly expanded now and all kinds of people visit.

Yuppies and politicos seem to drop by for the cocktail hour, and a flavorful mix of New Yorkers and out-of-towners come for dinner.

I remember one evening sitting there with Jimmy Breslin, having a drink and talking. It's a great place to go for sports talk.

The steaks are great, too, Steve.

Ryan McFadden, 800 2nd Avenue at 42nd Street, New York, N.Y. 10017. Telephone: 212/599-2226. Reservations recommended but not required. Hours: 11:30 a.m.-3 a.m. Monday-Friday; noon-4 p.m. brunch Saturday-Sunday; 5 p.m.-midnight dinner Saturday-Sunday. Credit cards: American Express, Diner's Club. Personal checks accepted only from persons known to proprietors. Price range: Entrées $6-$11, lunch; $8-$15, dinner. Bar service. Getting there: The restaurant is two blocks east of Grand Central Station, one block west from the United Nations Building.

VEGETABLE CONSOMMÉ

3 ounces onions
2 ounces carrots
1 ounce celery
1 ounce butter
1 quart hot chicken stock
2 ounces tomatoes, chopped
½ ounce peas
Salt and white pepper

Cut vegetables uniformly and finely. Sauté onions, carrots and celery lightly in butter. Add stock and tomatoes to other vegetables and simmer. Skim fat.

When vegetables are done, remove from heat. Remove as much fat as possible. Adjust seasonings.

Immediately before serving, add peas.

STEAMED MUSSELS WITH TOMATO BROTH

5 dozen mussels
1 dozen plum tomatoes
1 cup white wine
3 tablespoons tomato paste
1 ounce Pernod
1 pinch basil
1 pinch oregano

Clean and beard mussels thoroughly. Using large steaming pot, slowly stir tomatoes, wine, tomato paste, Pernod, basil and oregano to simmer.

Put mussels in broth and steam for approximately 6 - 7 minutes (or until the mussel shells open). Serve immediately with Italian bread to enjoy full flavor of broth.

RYAN McFADDEN'S STUFFED STEAK

6 (10-ounce) aged sirloin
shell steaks
6 cloves garlic, minced
12 ounces Gruyere cheese,
sliced
6 ounces prosciutto

Butterfly each steak by slicing approximately a 3-inch pocket in fat side of steak. Inside each steak pocket, insert 1 clove garlic, salt and pepper to taste. Add 2 ounces cheese and 1 ounce prosciutto in each pocket.

Grill as desired.

Note: For medium-well or well, grill to rare before inserting cheese and ham.

GARLIC MASHED POTATOES

3 heads garlic
4 tablespoons butter
1 cup boiling milk
2 tablespoons flour
⅛ teaspoon pepper
2½ pounds baking potatoes
3-4 tablespoons whipping
cream

Separate garlic into cloves. Drop into boiling water 2 minutes, drain and peel. Cook garlic and butter in covered saucepan 20 minutes or until tender. Don't brown. Blend in flour for 2 minutes; don't brown. Beat in milk and seasonings. Simmer gently while stirring. Purée garlic mixture in blender or sieve.

Peel and quarter potatoes. Cook until tender, drain and mash. Place potatoes in saucepan and stir several minutes for moisture to evaporate. If skin begins to form on bottom of pan, remove from heat.

Beat in 1 or 2 tablespoons more softened butter, 1 tablespoon at a time. Add salt and pepper. Beat hot garlic sauce vigorously into the hot potatoes. Beat in cream slowly to thin to desired consistency.

SAUTÉED BUTTER-GLAZED CARROTS

3 pounds carrots
3 cups beef stock
4 tablespoons sugar
Pinch pepper
12 tablespoons butter
4 tablespoons parsley, minced

Simmer carrots slowly in uncovered saucepan with stock, sugar, pepper and butter until carrots are just tender and liquid has reduced to syrupy glaze. If carrots are cooked before glaze is formed, remove carrots and reduce stock. Correct seasoning.

Reheat just before serving and roll carrots gently in pan to coat with syrup. Sprinkle with parsley.

JIMMY V's GRAND MARNIER SOUFFLÉ

1 pint milk
4 ounces butter
4 ounces flour
3 or 4 oranges, juice and grated rind
2 fluid ounces Grand Marnier
7 egg yolks
6 egg whites
2 ounces sugar

Bring milk to boil. Mix butter and flour to paste. Add paste to milk over low flame gradually and stir with wooden spoon until mixture thickens and returns to boil.

Remove from heat. Turn mixture into a bowl. While stirring with wooden spoon, add rinds, then juice, then Grand Marnier gradually to mixture.

Gradually add yolks to mixture (a couple at a time) while stirring with wooden spoon. Allow mixture to cool. This batter will combine with egg whites and sugar.

Whip egg whites to very light peaks. Add sugar gradually while continuing to whip to soft peak. Stir ¼ of whites into batter mixture. Fold in remaining whites.

Place batter in buttered and sugared containers. Bake in preheated 400-degree oven approximately 15 minutes.

THE FISH MARKET

Amawalk, N.Y.

DINNER FOR TWO

Hot Antipasto
Seafood Paella
Tossed Mixed Salad
Fresh Fruit in Season

Wine: White or red, either
Pinot Grigio or St. Emilion

You talk about the camaraderie that comes from eating great food. This place takes it to an art form.

You can count on waiting an hour or two outside before you get a table inside. But that's part of the fun. You don't go with people who want to slip the maitre d' $10 or $100 to get seated immediately or to get a better seat. You go with people who want to make an evening of it.

The Fish Market is out in the country in Amawalk, N.Y., in an old two-story house. As you come up, you see tanks of live lobsters and trout on the front lawn. Just pick out the one you want cooked to order.

Chef and owner John Conti prepares your order with olive oil, fresh butter or wine and serves it with fresh salads, breads and fruits.

And while you are waiting for your table, you can order shrimp and beer and they will bring it outside where everybody's sitting on tree trunks or around the tables there. And you make a lot of new friends while you're waiting.

Everytime a special couple would come to visit us from some place we'd lived in the past—Rutgers, Johns Hopkins, Bucknell—we'd take them there.

It's a chance to really catch up on a relationship.

When you get inside, I'm really talking great seafood. The floors are spread with sawdust and the dining tables are covered with newspapers. You don't have to worry about spills—just about whether you can hold all you'll want to eat.

The Fish Market, Box 325, Amawalk, N.Y. 10501.   Telephone: 914/245-4388.   Reservations not accepted. Hours: noon-2:30 p.m. and 6-9:30 p.m. seven days a week. Open all year.   Credit cards not accepted. Traveler's checks and personal checks accepted.   Bar service.   Getting there: The restaurant is on Route 35, six miles from Katonah and Highway 684 in the Amawalk section of Yorktown, near the Amawalk Dam.

12 mussels, cleaned
1 (1½ - 2 pounds) lobster
¼ pound bay scallops
4 medium shrimp, peeled and cleaned
1 medium can Italian tomatoes
½ cup red wine
Olive oil
8 -10 garlic cloves, chopped
Salt and pepper
Parsley, chopped

Marinara sauce was first made on Italian sailing ships. It was a quick sauce because the ship galley was so small and the sauce was made on short order. The name marinara sauce comes from mariner's sauce.

Parboil lobster in pot of boiling water for 2 minutes. Remove from pot. Cut down middle from claws to tail, using large kitchen shears. Cut each half into 4 pieces.

Crush tomatoes with hands. Add salt, pepper and wine. Heat oil, enough to cover bottom of pan plus a little more for 2 minutes. Add garlic, sauté until brown. Add seasoned oil to tomatoes; stir. Freshly chopped Italian parsley may be added if desired. Makes 1 pint marinara sauce. Keeps uncooked refrigerated 1 week.

Simmer marinara sauce in large pan 15 minutes. Add mussels and lobster pieces. Cover and cook until mussels open, 6 - 8 minutes. Add scallops and cook 2 minutes, covered. Add shrimp and cook 1 minute, covered. Serve in large bowl.

SEAFOOD PAELLA

2 pints marinara sauce
½ pint clam juice
6 littleneck clams or
6 cherrystone clams
12 mussels, cleaned
1 lobster, parboiled and
cut in pieces
Crab in shell, king, blue claw or
snow or combination, in
desired amount
4 cups parboiled rice
4 medium filets of sole or
flounder
½ cup bay scallops
3 medium shrimp, peeled
and cleaned
2 onions, chopped
2 green peppers, chopped
2 sweet red peppers, chopped

Paella comes from the name of the pan in which the dish is cooked. It is large, round and shallow with 2 "ears" or handles. A large frying pan may be used instead of a paella pan.

Fill paella pan or large frying pan half way with marinara sauce and clam juice. Add vegetables and clams. Simmer 2 minutes or until clams begin to open. Add mussels, lobster, crab and rice. Place filets, rolled, and scallops on top of rice. Cover and cook 3 minutes. Add shrimp. Cover and cook 3 minutes.

Spoon out clams and mussels gently from bottom of pan. Spoon out some of broth so there is not too much remaining in pan. Place clams and mussels on top of fish and scallops. Serve from same dish.

Note: Do not use saffron on paella made with fresh fish. Saffron was used for its pungency when leftover meat and fish were used to make this dish.

TOSSED MIXED SALAD

Combine a variety of green lettuce in season and serve with choice of dresssing. A combination of iceberg, romaine, chickory and red leaf lettuce is pleasing.

FRESH FRUIT

For dessert, serve clean, fresh fruit in season. Choices may include apples, pears, grapefruit, oranges, tangerines, watermelon, plums, etc. We will serve a whole apple in a bowl and provide a knife.

VELLEGGIA'S

Baltimore, Md.

DINNER FOR TWO

Vongole al Bagno
Fettucine in Butter Sauce
Veal Saltimbocca
Broccoli, Italian Style
Zabaglione

Wine: Pinot Grigio or Soave

Baltimore's got all kinds of great restaurants, but whenever my Mom and Dad would come to visit us while we lived there, we'd go to Velleggia's.

Enrico Velleggia opened a tavern way back in 1934 to supplement the income he earned as a stone mason. His wife, Maria, started cooking meals for the people who came, and now they've got three dining rooms, a banquet room and a bar.

Just shows you what we Italians can do once we get started.

Maria still directs the cooking, but the Velleggia sons, Frank and Naz, and their kids, now run the place. It's in Baltimore's Little Italy and is plainly a family-run restaurant even though it's gotten a little bit more uptown.

The food is terrific. I remember the garlic bread especially for some reason. You know—crusty and with enough zip to keep vampires away for months afterwards.

The waitresses are the kind who can take the order of a party of 10, keep it all in their heads and serve everyone perfectly.

It was our family spot away from New York.

Velleggia's, 204 South High Street, Baltimore, Md. 21202. Telephone: 301/685-2620. Reservations recommended but not required. Hours: 11:30 a.m. - midnight Sunday-Thursday; 11:30 a.m. - 3 a.m. Friday-Saturday. Closed December 24-26. Credit cards: VISA, MasterCard, American Express, Choice. Price range: Entrées $5 and up. Bar service. Getting there: From the Inner Harbor, take Pratt Street east approximately three blocks to Little Italy.

VONGOLE AL BAGNO

16 small clams in shell,
littlenecks or very small
cherrystones
2 tablespoons olive oil
2 cloves garlic, minced fine
½ small onion, minced
Salt
Black pepper
Red pepper
Oregano
½ teaspoon basil, minced
¾ cup chicken broth
1 ounce dry white wine

Scrub clams in shell in clean water; set aside.

In 6-quart saucepan, sauté garlic and onion in olive oil. Add pinch of salt, black pepper, red pepper and oregano. Stir in basil, chicken broth and wine. Add the clams and simmer, uncovered, about 15 minutes or until clams open about ¼ inch.

Serve clams in au gratin or other dish with sides. Pour little broth over them. Place plain or garlic toast points on side.

FETTUCINE IN BUTTER SAUCE

½ pound fettucine noodles
1 pint cream
2 ounces butter
1 cup Parmesan or Fontina
cheese, grated
Freshly ground pepper

Cook noodles in 2 quarts boiling water with 1 teaspoon salt until *al dente*. Drain.

In 5-quart saucepan, heat cream and butter to melt butter. Add cheese and continue to heat until cheese melts and sauce thickens. Add freshly ground pepper to taste. Remove ¾ sauce. Add noodles to remaining sauce, tossing well to coat in sauce. Place noodles on serving dish. Pour sauce over top.

VEAL SALTIMBOCCA

2 (¼-inch thick, 5-ounce) veal steaks
2 slices mozzarella cheese
2 slices prosciutto
Salt
Pepper
2 tablespoons butter
1 teaspoon lemon juice
1 teaspoon olive oil
2 tablespoons Marsala
2 tablespoons chicken broth

Place veal on cutting board and pound to tenderize and make thinner. Salt and pepper each steak.

Place cheese and prosciutto on each steak. Folds sides in, letter style, tucking in edges of each end. Press the folds.

In medium-size frying pan, melt butter. Flour 1 side of veal. Fry veal with floured side down until golden, 2-3 minutes. Do not overcook. Turn and add lemon juice, olive oil, Marsala and chicken broth. Cook 2-3 minutes to reduce sauce. Serve veal on platter with sauce.

BROCCOLI, ITALIAN STYLE

A side dish recommended for this menu is fresh broccoli, cut up and cooked lightly in a frying pan with olive oil and garlic.

ZABAGLIONE

1 egg, plus 1 egg yolk
2 heaping tablespoons sugar
2 tablespoons Marsala
Rind of 1 lemon, grated

In top of double-boiler, combine all ingredients. Beat mixture until it begins to thicken and become frothy. Place pot in or over hot water and beat 3 - 4 minutes or until thick and foamy. Pour into stemmed glasses. May serve over sweet pears or with wafer cookie.

CASA NICOLO

Raleigh, N.C.

DINNER FOR FOUR

Stuffed Mushrooms
Stracciatella
Linguine Primavera
Veal Florentina
Radicchio and Fennel
Zabaglione

Wine: A dry white wine or Soave

When I came to North Carolina, the entire Italian-American population greeted me. That was wonderful. Then me and Angela went out and had pizza.

Actually, there are a lot of good Italian restaurants in Raleigh, but most of them are owned by Greeks—some of whom are my very good friends.

I guess Raleigh's Casa Nicolo, though, has a special meaning for me because the first time I went was when Lou Pucillo, one of NCSU's former great basketball players and an Italian, of course, had a dinner there for me and my staff.

I met a whole bunch of folks in the local Italian-American club there, too.

Then Nick Sarrocco, who's the owner and operator of Casa Nicolo, catered a big $100-a-head dinner for the Wolfpack Club. What can you say but something nice about a guy like that?

Nick serves more than pizza and pasta. It's where I take people when I want to say, "Now, that's Italian."

Casa Nicolo, 1733 North Boulevard, Raleigh, N.C. 27604. Telephone: 919/828-9988. Reservations recommended but not required. Hours: 4-11 p.m. Monday-Saturday. Closed all major holidays. Credit cards: All major credit cards. Price range: Average entrée is $8. Bar service. Getting there: Take the Farmers Market Exit from the Beltline (Highways 1 and 64) onto Downtown Boulevard. Turn left at the Milner Inn. The restaurant is on the right.

STUFFED MUSHROOMS

12 large mushroom caps, cleaned
1 cup bread crumbs
1 tablespoon fresh parsley, chopped
2 tablespoons Romano cheese, grated
½ teaspoon garlic, minced
1 tablespoon onion, chopped
2 ounces olive oil
4 ounces water
Pinch salt
Pinch pepper

Combine bread crumbs, parsley, cheese, garlic, onion, olive oil and water. Distribute this filling evenly in mushroom caps.

Place filled caps in greased baking dish. Bake in preheated 350-degree oven 20 minutes or until brown.

STRACCIATELLA

8 ounces chicken stock
2 ribs celery, sliced
1 large onion, chopped
1 large carrot, sliced
6 cups water
½ teaspoon whole green peppercorns
3 large eggs, beaten
2/3 cup Romano cheese, grated
2 tablespoons fresh parsley, minced
¼ teaspoon salt

Combine chicken stock, celery, carrot, onion and water. Bring to rolling boil.

Combine peppercorns, eggs, cheese, parsley and salt. Pour mixture into boiling liquid. Remove from heat and serve.

LINGUINE PRIMAVERA

1 pound linguine
20 ounces white sauce made
with heavy cream
8 clams
8 shrimp
8 mussels
8 ounces carrots, cut in
julienne strips
8 ounces zucchini, cut in
julienne strips

Prepare white sauce. Set aside.

Cook linguine *al dente*. Drain and set aside.

Combine white sauce, clams, shrimp, mussels, carrots and zucchini. Cook until seafood is done and vegetables are crisp-tender, 5-10 minutes. Serve sauce over linguine.

VEAL FLORENTINA

1 pound (4 4-ounce) veal
cutlets, pounded thin
4 teaspoons butter, clarified
8 ounces white wine
4 ounces chicken demi-glace
(stock)
4 ounces marinara sauce
1 ounce lemon juice
8 ounces fresh spinach
Pinch salt
Pinch pepper

Steam spinach until done. Drain. Set aside but keep warm.

Melt butter in skillet. Add veal and sauté on both sides until lightly browned, 2-3 minutes. Add wine, chicken stock, marinara sauce, lemon, salt and pepper. Heat through, 1-2 minutes.

Top each cutlet with spinach. Spoon pan juices over, if desired. Serve.

RADICCHIO & FENNEL SALAD

12 Italian black olives, pitted
¼ cup olive oil
2 tablespoons lemon juice
1 flat anchovy, chopped
Pinch salt
Pinch black pepper
1 fresh fennel bulb
1 head radicchio

Combine olives, olive oil, lemon juice, anchovy, salt and pepper.

Break fennel bulb and radicchio into bite-size pieces. Toss with dressing.

Note: Endive may be substituted for radicchio.

ZABAGLIONE

5 large eggs, beaten
¼ cup sugar
½ cup Amaretto liqueur
¼ cup dry white wine

Combine all ingredients. Whip with a whisk over heat until mixture is firm but not stiff. Serve immediately.

GUARINO'S

Cary, N.C.

DINNER FOR TWO

Clams Casino
Vegetable Soup
Pollo Alla Mozzarella
Risotto
Ice Cream

Wine: Ruffino Orvietto Classico
white wine, chilled

You've heard about these great restaurants that are just a little bit out of the way?

Well, Guarino's in Cary is like that. It's so out of the way, it's underneath a gas station. No kidding.

Nick Guarino and his wife are super people. Not only is he a gourmet chef, when you eat at his restaurant, it's like going to visit your parents.

My kids come in and the baby sits up front and puts the credit cards through the machine. She gets to act like a waitress.

They always have a little doll for her or a gift of some sort.

Guarino prepares his own salad dressings, breads, sauces and many of the pastas. He goes back to the way our grandparents did things in the kitchen.

But you get more than a wonderful meal here. You get great friendship. You go away with so much more than you brought.

Guarino's, 1501 Buck Jones Road, Cary, N.C. 27606. Telephone: 919/469-8877. Hours: 4:30-9:30 p.m. Monday-Thursday; 4:30-11 p.m. Friday-Saturday. Closed Sunday and all major holidays. Credit cards: VISA, MasterCard, American Express. Personal checks accepted from immediate area. Getting there: From Beltline (Highways 1 and 64), take Buck Jones Exit, turn onto Buck Jones Road, take first entrance to South Hills Shopping Center on the right. Turn to right. Restaurant on the lower level under the gas station.

CLAMS CASINO

8 fresh clams, shucked and cleaned under cold running water
½ small green pepper, chopped fine
Bacon, uncooked, cubed, to cover clams
Olive oil
Oregano

Place clams in warm water to get shells to open. Shuck and clean clams. Place in casserole dish.

Sprinkle each clam with enough olive oil to coat it. Cover clams with bacon. Add green pepper. Place a pinch of oregano on each clam.

Bake in preheated 450-degree oven 10-15 minutes or until bacon crisps.

VEGETABLE SOUP

2 ribs celery, chopped fine
2-3 carrots, sliced fine
3 scallions, heads and green stem, or onion, chopped fine
1 teaspoon parsley
1 teaspoon chicken base or bouillon
1 teaspoon beef base or bouillon
1 tablespoon Parmesan cheese, grated
Salt
¼ teaspoon white pepper
1½ quarts water

Combine all ingredients, bring to a boil and simmer 60 minutes.

POLO ALLA MOZZARELLA

2 (4-ounce) chicken breasts
¼ teaspoon parsley
¼ teaspoon oregano
Dash garlic powder
¼ teaspoon rosemary
1 cup water, divided
1/3 cup mushrooms, sliced
¼ cup celery, thin-sliced
¼ cup onion, sliced
½ tablespoon butter
2 capsful sherry wine
2 slices mozzarella
2 links Italian sausage, sliced
and cooked

Mix together parsley, oregano, garlic powder, rosemary and ½ cup water. Place chicken breasts in pan, cover with mixture, and bake in preheated 450-degree oven 15 minutes.

Combine mushrooms, celery, onion, butter, remaining water and sherry in a covered pan. Simmer for 20 minutes. Pour sauce over chicken. Place mozzarella on chicken. Add sausage.

Bake for 15 minutes in 450-degree oven.

RISOTTO

1 cup rice, cooked
2 tablespoons Parmesan cheese,
grated
1-2 ounces butter
Black pepper
Fresh parsley, chopped fine
Olive oil

Cook the cup of rice in 2 cups water until done.

Combine cooked rice, cheese, butter, pepper and parsley.

Heat olive oil, stir in the rice mixture, and heat through.

ICE CREAM

Vanilla ice cream
1 ounce Drambuie
Whipped cream
Maraschino cherries

Place ice cream in a bowl, Pour Drambuie over. Top with whipped cream and a cherry.

Serve the ice cream with espresso coffee. Provide lemon slices on the side. Squeeze lemon slice over the coffee and then drop the slice into the coffee.

THE CRAB SHACK

Salter Path, N.C.

DINNER FOR FOUR

Steamed Crabs
Shrimp or Scallops Sautéed in Butter
Captain Salad
Cole Slaw
French Fries or Baked Potato

There are very few places I can get away to, where I can say that just the thought of it conjures relaxation and fun.

The Crab Shack in Salter Path is one of them.

We have a house down at Atlantic Beach, and when we're down there I eat almost every meal at The Crab Shack. I love crabs and I love *their* crabs.

The people are so nice that last Christmas when my assistant asked, they sent five dozen hard-shell crabs up to Raleigh so I could eat them here.

But they're not kidding when they say it's a shack. The building used to be a fish house and outside the restaurant is modest in the extreme.

Inside you get fresh steamed crab and fresh vegetables and fried mushrooms and shrimp in their shells and ... You won't even have time for the Bon Appetit before you start.

The Crab Shack, Box 101, Salter Path, N.C. 28575.   Telephone: 919/247-3444.   Hours: 11 a.m.- 10 p.m. seven days a week. Closed for Christmas.   Credit cards: VISA, MasterCard.   Price range: Entrées $5.25 - $8.95.   Getting there: On Highway 58 from Atlantic Beach, turn right at Salter Path Methodist Church; from Emerald Isle, turn left at the church. Restaurant on right just after the turn.

STEAMED CRABS

3-4 dozen live blue crabs
½ gallon water
1 cup vinegar
Crab Shack Seafood Seasoning
or Old Bay

Place seafood steaming pot on top of stove. Pour water and vinegar in the pot. Layer crabs one dozen at a time above the water. Sprinkle seafood seasoning over crabs as you layer them.

Put the lid on the pot and cook on high heat for 20 minutes. Delicious served with crackers or hush puppies and melted butter.

SHRIMP OR SCALLOPS SAUTÉED IN BUTTER

Scallops or shrimp
(peeled and deveined)
Butter or margarine

Place enough butter or margarine to cover bottom of fry pan and heat until melted. Add scallops or shrimp.

Sauté on medium heat, stirring constantly until seafood is well heated. Do not overcook, this will cause seafood to become tough. Serve with your favorite vegetables and hush puppies for a mouth watering meal.

CAPTAIN SALAD

Crisp green lettuce
Tomato wedges
Green peppers
Cucumber, sliced
Carrots, shredded
Radishes, sliced
Green onions
Cauliflower
Boiled shrimp
Crabmeat
Dressing of your choice

Cut lettuce in a bowl. Add peppers, cucumbers, carrots, radishes, onions and cauliflower. Toss until well mixed. Add tomato wedges.

Sprinkle with shrimp and crab meat.

Pour on your favorite dressing. Serve with crackers.

COLE SLAW

You can use one of the recipes from the preceding section.

FRENCH FRIES/BAKED POTATO

These two ways of preparing potatoes are so standard that no recipes are necessary. Use your own preferred method for whichever you desire.

GULLYFIELD'S

Myrtle Beach, S.C.

DINNER FOR FOUR

Alaskan Crab Legs
She-Crab Soup
Fresh Garden Salad
Baked Stuffed Shrimp
Hot Peppermint Patty

I didn't know what Southern low-country seafood was until I hit Gullyfield's where you get seafood and vegetables and breads and desserts a la South Carolina.

The Myrtle Beach restaurant is owned by John Rhodes, who's a friend of the Atlantic Coast Conference. He has a number of restaurants, including Gullyfield's, which does an enormous volume of business.

And it was there where I first caught the spirit of the ACC. We were having the ACC summer meetings. John closed the restaurant except for ACC meeting participants. That was when I got one of my first real feelings of being in the ACC.

Now I never go to the Myrtle Beach area without stopping by.

Gullyfield's is a yellow frame house with a big porch. It's located on a two-acre lake and you can see the alligators bobbing for the hush puppies visitors throw to them. They don't call it the low country for nothing.

Gullyfield's, Box 7276, Myrtle Beach, S.C. 29577. Telephone: 803/449-3111. Hours: 5-10 p.m. seven days a week. Open from March 1 to mid-November. Reservations for large groups only Monday-Friday. Credit cards: VISA, Carte Blanche, American Express, MasterCard, Bank Americard. Personal checks not accepted. Price range: Entrées $9.95-$21.95. Bar service. Getting there: The restaurant is on "Restaurant Row," on Highway 17 North.

ALASKAN CRAB LEGS

4 clusters of crab legs
(1 cluster per serving)

Drop crab legs in hot water or place in steamer until piping hot (approximately 10 minutes). Split each leg and serve with hot butter.

SHE-CRAB SOUP

Harris she-crab soup base
½ cup milk
¾ cup backfin crab meat
Sherry
Half and half

Combine soup base, milk and crab and warm. Place in cups; add 1 teaspoon sherry to each. Top with 1 teaspoon half and half. Place under broiler until cream blisters.

FRESH GARDEN SALAD

Use your own favorite combination of garden-fresh vegetables and salad dressings.

BAKED STUFFED SHRIMP

16 jumbo shrimp
(4 per serving)
1 pound "special" crab meat
2 tablespoons bell pepper,
minced
2 tablespoons onion, minced
2 eggs
½ stick butter
1 tablespoon Poupon mustard
2 teaspoons Worcestershire
sauce
½ cup milk

Butterfly cleaned and deveined shrimp. Thoroughly blend crab meat and remaining ingredients to stuff each shrimp.

Place under broiler approximately 10 minutes. Serve with hot butter.

HOT PEPPERMINT PATTY

1 cup hot chocolate
1 shot white creme de menthe
Whipped cream
Chocolate sprinkles

To make this after-dinner drink, combine hot chocolate and cream de menthe, and top with whipped cream and chocolate sprinkles.

A TOUCH OF CLASS

Seattle, Wash.

DINNER FOR FOUR

Soup of the Day
Arroz Guacho
Chicken Delynn
Mixed Salad
French Bread
Sundae

Wine: A Johannisberg Riesling

We weren't in the 1984 NCAA finals in Seattle, but that didn't keep me from hearing about one of Seattle's finest restaurants when I went out to see the game between the University of Houston and Georgetown University.

A Touch of Class puts together a restaurant and a disco. Yep. You heard it right. Disco may have gone out in some places, but the beat has gone on for 15 years at A Touch of Class.

You get a light show and stainless steel dance floors. Only basketball is more fun.

After you dance, you can dine to the sound of a waterfall. Salmon, of course, is a house specialty. Chef Wilbur Monturiol is also known for the delicious dishes he creates from ocean-fresh garden prawns—large shrimp found in the water off the coast of Mexico. Monturiol has a special touch with the poultry and oriental dishes, and the restaurant offers prime rib and steak for beef lovers.

A Touch Of Class, 156 Southwest 152nd Street, Seattle, Wash. 98166.   Telephone: 206/243-1800. Reservations recommended but not required.   Hours: 5-10 p.m. Tuesday-Saturday. Closed Sunday-Monday and all major holidays.   Credit cards: MasterCard, VISA. Personal checks accepted.   Price range: Entrées $7-$19.   Bar service.   Getting there: The restaurant is located one mile west of the Sea-Tac (Seattle-Tacoma) Airport in the heart of Burien.

SOUP OF THE DAY

This course varies according to which ingredients the chef has on hand each day. He uses no specific recipe, bringing to bear his creativity and cooking skills. You may wish to use one of your favorite recipes.

ARROZ GUACHO

2 cups uncooked
long-grain rice
¼ pound butter
1 potato, peeled and diced
1 carrot, diced
1 green pepper, diced
2 stalks celery, diced
½ onion, diced
6 green olives, pitted
1 tomato, diced
1 sprig cilantro
¼ teaspoon cumin seed
1 bay leaf
1 small chicken, cut in pieces
5 cups chicken broth
½ teaspoon chicken base
1 tablespoon vinegar
¼ tablespoon white pepper
Salt to taste
1 drop yellow food coloring
(optional)

Rinse rice in water to remove all starch.

Melt butter in saucepan over medium heat. Add rice and stir until very hot.

Add potato, carrot, green pepper, celery, onion, olives, tomato, cilantro, cumin seed, bay leaf and chicken. Cook until onion is translucent.

Add broth, chicken base, vinegar, pepper and salt. Cook until rice is fluffy and chicken is tender. If desired, add food coloring before serving.

Note: Arroz Guacho may be served as a meal in itself, or served with Chicken Delynn. (In the latter case, you may want to remove the chicken used to flavor the Arroz Guacho, and save it for a future meal.)

CHICKEN DELYNN

1 tablespoon soy sauce
1 teaspoon salt
1 teaspoon white pepper
1 ounce honey
3 cups water
1 egg yolk
1 teaspoon monosodium
glutamate (MSG)
4 boneless chicken breasts
(cutlets)
4 slices lean ham
8 slices Swiss cheese
1 cup flour, sifted
1 package Panko
(Japanese breading)
6 tablespoons flour (to toast)
6 tablespoons chicken fat
2 cups chicken broth
2 dashes poultry seasoning
2 pinches dry parsley
2 cups sesame oil
4 ounces slivered almonds

To make marinade, combine soy sauce, salt, pepper, honey and water. While stirring, add egg yolk and MSG. Set aside.

Remove skin of chicken breasts carefully. Do not tear meat. With mallet, tenderize meat, beginning at one corner. Spread blows lightly along the edge, feathering the perimeter. Pound in the middle just enough to make a thin sheet, 6 inches square and ¼ inch thick.

For each cutlet, take a slice of ham and a slice of cheese, place them together and fold them in half. Put in middle of cutlet, and fold so no ham or cheese is visible.

Dip in marinade, then in flour, then back in marinade and, finally, in Japanese breading. Coat cutlets completely, and set aside.

Toast 6 tablespoons of flour in saucepan. Remove from heat as soon as flour turns light brown. Add 6 tablespoons of chicken fat. Mix well until a smooth paste is formed. Set aside.

In separate pan, bring chicken broth to boil, and add flour paste a little at a time until this sauce has a smooth consistency. Add poultry seasoning and parsley. Set aside, and keep hot.

Heat sesame oil to 325 degrees. Cook breaded cutlets 3-5 minutes. Turn over and cook another 2 minutes. Remove. Immediately place 1 slice of cheese over each cutlet. Place in serving dish. Smother with sauce. Sprinkle with slivered almonds.

Note: Chicken Delynn is named for Delynn Scott, who co-owns A Touch of Class with her father, Gene Keyton.

MIXED SALAD

The restaurant offers a salad bar with over 40 items from which to choose. The diner will find both familiar items such as raisin-carrot salad and cottage cheese (from a local dairy) and the unique such as pickled, crinkle-cut red beets in apple vinegar. Several choices of dressings and toppings provide the finishing touches to this course.

Create your own salad bar in your home by serving a variety of fresh vegetables, toppings and choice of dressings. These could include cherry tomatos or tomato wedges, fresh mushroom slices, green pepper strips, cucumber slices, broccoli florets, chopped hard-boiled egg, shredded cheese, bacon bits and bean sprouts. Look in your pantry and see what other ideas come to mind.

FRENCH BREAD

Fresh-baked bread comes with each meal. The restaurant serves half-loaves of French bread. These come from a local bakery. You may choose to make your own bread or purchase French or sourdough bread at a local bakery.

This course allows the kid in everyone to have some fun. The restaurant has a soft ice cream machine. Diners may choose vanilla or chocolate, and as much or as little as they want. The ice cream comes from a local dairy. To top the ice cream you will find chocolate and strawberry sauces, candy-coated chopped nuts, maraschino cherries and whipped cream.

You can have just as much fun in your own home with a make-your-own sundae. Provide two or more choices of ice cream and toppings and allow your guests to express themselves. You may want to try the chocolate sauce recipe in the first section of this book.

THREE MEN WHO TAUGHT ME THE BUSINESS

My lifelong love affair with hoops probably began in the cradle, maybe while my Dad was regaling me with nightly reports of his exploits moonlighting as a professional basketball player in the old professional basketball league. (He also at one time played semi-pro baseball while teaching health and physical education and coaching full-time in the New York City parochial school system.)

Dad bought me my first kid-sized basketball, football and baseball and bat when I was still a toddler, and I remember him spending at least an hour most days teaching my older brother Nick and me how to shoot baskets, throw a football or hit a baseball. And he spent this special time with us even though he was probably juggling two or three jobs, trying to support the family.

From my father, all three of us learned a *love* for the game of basketball and a love of coaching. My brother Nick, who is now with Wang in New York City, coached for 12 years before he took a job in business. And my brother Bobby, who is currently head basketball coach at St. Francis of Brooklyn, has also made coaching a career.

So, from my Dad, I got my passion for the game. When people say I seem to be very active and emotional at games, I really got that from my father. He could throw a clipboard with the best of them!

But with that *passion* for the game, I also got a certain *compassion* for the players. When I got my first job in coaching, my father said to me: "You'll be a good coach if you can remember this: Your players need you *more* when you lose than when you win."

And that I've never forgotten. He always made a point, after a loss, of coming down to the locker room and making sure he talked with each kid and gave him a little pat, you know, and got him all juiced up again. And after a win, the kids are usually pretty happy, so you can be a little more low-profile.

My Dad always stressed that playing ball should be *fun*. He told me and the other kids he coached at Seaford High School: "If you're not enjoying yourself, don't even stay on the team. Don't play. Because we're going to have *fun*.

"I want to win," he said, "but if we don't win, it's really not that important. It's *how* you win or lose that will bother me."

We were talking about this recently and he explained, "Some of the kids I coached would get to the point where they would be completely negative if we lost. It was never *them*. It was always the referee; it was always somebody else. They never took stock of themselves and said, 'Wait a minute. Maybe *I* wasn't that good.'

"So I used to tell the kids: 'Look, you can *win* and I'll chew you out. And you can *lose* and I'll pat you on the back and say you played the very best you could.'"

If I got my passion for the game and compassion for the people who play it from my Dad, I learned the *business* of the game from Bill Foster, who was my coach at Rutgers University. Later he coached at Duke University in Durham, N.C., and is now head basketball coach at the University of South Carolina at Columbia. He was at Rutgers all six years I was there, first as a player and then two years as one of his assistant coaches.

Bill Foster was—and is—a tremendously *organized* person who left nothing— NOTHING—to chance. He was a great model for a young player like me who wanted to become a coach: He was an excellent X-and-O man, very well versed in recruiting and a good teacher—as well as an excellent businessman.

He was one other thing which I emulate which I shouldn't—he was a *workaholic*. He had a tremendous work ethic, and he was always working on so many different things at the same time. Plus, he's a good family man, too, although I'm sure his family—as mine has—suffered at times.

So, from Bill Foster, I learned a tremendous organizational ability and business sense. And, yet, he always took care of his players. If you look back, he always hired his former players as assistants.

He was very loyal to his own players, afterwards; and I have always remained very close to him.

The third man who schooled me in the fine points of college coaching is Dee Rowe, under whom I served as an assistant while he was head coach at the University of Connecticut in Storrs. (He has since retired from coaching, and now works for the university in fund-raising and alumni affairs areas.)

Dee's style of coaching combined the passion that I inherited from my father with the understanding of the intricacies of the game and the business sense I learned from Bill Foster. Dee was the epitome of the man who coaches almost solely with emotion, on emotion. And he is a great, great speaker; and I'd go to meetings with him and he'd get up and give great, *inspiring* talks. And he has a great style about him and he was very motivational in his approach to the game; but he was also the type of guy who was great with *all* of the people in a program.

In other words, sometimes when you're the head coach, and you've got 12,000 people out there and the media and all that, you'll get *short* if, say, the equipment man or the trainer has fouled up something.

Dee never did. Dee would always say, "Everyone has his own job to do, and everybody's job is as important as everybody else's. And you should respect that."

You know, he had that ability to deal with the president of a major corporation and then go and have coffee with anybody in the organization. I'll tell you a great example: We were scouting Yale my first year at Connecticut, and they were playing Fordham. At the end of the game, I couldn't find Dee. And he was talking to one of the maintenance people about what a great job the guy had done on the floor, telling him that it really looked terrific. Dee was wondering what he did with it and how he did it.

And it was a *genuine* interest; that's how Dee was.

It all ties together: my Dad's great passion for the game, his ability to really be close to the kids at that age and to put winning and losing in perspective; Bill Foster's professionalism, combined with an astute basketball mind, a care and concern for his athletes and business sense; and Dee's fervor for the game and his incredible ability to relate to *everybody* involved in our program.

When you put all that together, I'd like to think that's—in some respects—made me whatever it is I am today. I think it's a lot because of those three people.

THE USES OF ADVERSITY

People do not talk enough about failure. It is somehow taboo—even though we all experience it regularly in our daily lives.

Failure is something I talk about a lot when I speak to business groups. It is, in the words of Henry Ford, merely "the opportunity to begin again, more intelligently."

Many of the most important lessons that athletics teach you have to do with how to deal with failure, as well as success.

Learning how to cope with adversity, how to be successful *against* the odds, has helped me at every stage—as an athlete, as a coach and just as a person.

Although I won some honors as a high school basketball player, I was not heavily recruited. In fact, I was a walk-on at Rutgers University. I had to try out for the freshman basketball team. There were 110 people there, and it seemed like 80 of them were exactly my size—six feet tall. But I made that team, and played on the varsity the next three years. In fact, my senior year I was one of the co-captains on a team that won third place in the 1967 National Invitational Tournament—and I made first team, all tournament.

But I never had more than a partial scholarship while I was at Rutgers. Folks, you're looking at a guy who went to school and *paid* for it.

It would be different if my story was: great high school athlete, heavily recruited; chooses from 10 schools; goes on to become a superstar in college; leads his team to a national championship; starts coaching as an assistant in The Bigs; then becomes a head coach in The Bigs; has immediate success; and then wins the national championship. You go tell that story to a fellow who's out there struggling, and he can't relate to it.

I think what made N.C. State's Cinderella story so meaningful to so many was the fact that we did struggle, that we did overcome a lot of adversity—and that we did what the consensus of "experts" said couldn't be done.

People said that our winning the Atlantic Coast Conference championship was a fluke, that winning the first NCAA playoff games and the regionals were more flukes. Maybe some of the sportswriters hadn't noted that on N.C. State's way to the Final Four, starting with the ACC Tournament, we had beaten the University of North Carolina at Chapel Hill, the University of Virginia (twice) and the University of Nevada at Las Vegas—all ranked No. 1 at one time during the 1982-83 basketball season.

But even the writers who knew us, and knew our record, probably figured we had little chance to beat that awesome University of Houston team that had demolished a very fine University of Louisville team in the second game of the NCAA Semifinals.

Typical of press opinion before the championship game was columnist Dave Kindred's observation that "Trees will tap dance, elephants will ride in the Indianapolis 500 and Orson Welles will skip breakfast, lunch and dinner before State finds a way to beat Houston."

Were Akeem "The Dream" Olajuwon and the Houston Cougars invincible? In retrospect, we all know they were not. But my staff, my team and I knew it *then.* And although I was telling the media things like "if we get the opening tap, we may not take a shot until Tuesday," we *knew* we were going to be getting our shots, from the outside, from a Houston zone defense that let our premier long-range gunners—Dereck Whittenburg and Terry Gannon—bomb away from some of their favorite spots. And if Sidney Lowe got hot too, and if Thurl Bailey, Cozell McQueen and Lorenzo Charles held their own on the inside, well . . . we *could* win it.

I may have joked with the press; I may have told them we were going to hold the ball and play a slowdown game. But we knew different. Sure, our basic strategy was to try to dictate the *tempo* of the game, to cut down drastically on those runaway slam dunks that had broken Louisville's back. But we had a little offensive strategy of our own, too. I guess the ultimate irony of that game is that Dereck Whittenburg, who had made so many clutch shots for us all through his career, won worldwide fame with that air ball that Lorenzo grabbed under the basket and stuffed to beat Houston, 54-52.

Our winning N.C. State's second national championship on April 4, 1983 may have shocked the experts, but we thought we had a chance to win. After all, other than Houston, we were the only team playing that day.

I think we pushed Houston right down to the wire, and we did what I am always preaching to my players: We put ourselves in a *position to win*. And when it came down to the final seconds, we had the ball and the chance for the last shot — the last two, actually.

And The Dream came true, for the players, for the coaching staff, for the students, faculty and administrators, for the alumni and for the thousands of fans who had been behind us all along. Plus, this particular underdog's triumph against what was almost universally regarded as an unbeatable opponent has given thousands of people all around the country new hope that they can overcome the obstacles, the adversity, in their daily lives. I know because they have written me by the thousands to say our victory gave them new hope — and they're still writing.

I have always dreamed big dreams, and some of them have come true, too. First, I had a dream of playing guard on a college basketball team — and I *did*. Although, at first, I did not start on the freshman team, I did eventually work my way up to a starting role. And I started all three of my years on the varsity.

After I became a head coach, I had a dream of taking a team to Madison Square Garden where, as a kid, I had watched my Dad referee. And we *did*, even though it took 13 years.

The first time my Iona College team played the Garden, it was in a game with the University of South Florida — at 11 o'clock in the morning. They were still cleaning the joint, and the lights weren't on, but we were finally playing the Garden. And, just three years later, we were featured in the Main Event, playing the University of Louisville in the nine o'clock game. That was the year Darrell Griffith led them to the national championship; but the night *we* played, we beat them 77-60.

Dr. Robert Schuller has a book out called *Tough Times Never Last But Tough People Do!* I agree with that; and, heck, I could send him a chapter or two for his book about it because I lived through that. All of the adversity in my career as a player and a coach had prepared me for that moment when I stood before my team in Albuquerque, N.M.

People asked me later, Did I believe we could win? Hell, yes. Sure, I did. Because I had been living that, all those years.

When I went to Iona, people said, "You'll never have a *good* team!" But we *did*. They said we would never bring big-time college basketball to that little Catholic school. But we did that too.

And I had other goals. I wanted one of my teams to play in the nine o'clock game in Madison Square Garden. (It took me 13 years, but we did it.) And I wanted to win a national championship.

People always say, "You had it so good at Iona. Why did you leave?" Because I had accomplished my goals there, and wanted to pursue my ultimate goal of winning the NCAA Tournament.

People said, "You're crazy!" Well, that happened, too. But it wasn't easy.

The *real* story of N.C. State's 1983 championship team was that we did struggle, that we did have to cope with more than our fair share of adversity. But I was ready for that, because virtually my entire career as a player and coach had been spent overcoming obstacles, surmounting adversity—beating the odds by setting ambitious goals for myself and my players and teaching them that anything was possible if they just *believed* in their own abilities and the abilities of those around them to get the job done.

My recipe for success is simple: You take a healthy dose of dreams, and a pinch—or maybe even more of failure—and then a whole lot of persistence.

What I am saying is: Without the struggle, without the journey, without the adversity, without the failure, you never know the great joys; you just don't know the great achievements. You *need* to have some of those things happen to you.

I have learned a lot from winning basketball games. But losing has, perhaps, taught me more. Remember, it is the enthusiasm you bring to whatever you do, and the effort you make in your chosen profession, that count.

Set *higher* goals for yourself, dedicate yourself to achieving them—and you might be astonished at the results.

In any case, always remember what Teddy Roosevelt said about the "Battle of Life": "Far better it is to dare mighty things, to win glorious triumphs, even though checkered by failure, than to rank with those poor spirits who neither enjoy much nor suffer much, because they live in the gray twilight that knows not victory nor defeat."

MY FABULOUS POPCORN DIET

People have been trying for years to get me to reveal the secret of my famous popcorn diet. But I have always resisted making its particulars known ... until now. Because it's ridiculously simple. But it is also the type diet that you should not even begin without consulting your *physician*. (In fact, you should discuss any diet with your doctor before you start it.)

The foregoing, folks, is the type of warning I think every diet should have right up there in the first paragraph. In fact, the best ones do.

Now for the easy-to-follow directions for the Jim Valvano Popcorn Diet. First, you buy a hot-air popcorn popper and a bag or jar of your favorite brand of popping corn. Then, whenever you get hungry, you just pull out the old popper and pop as much as you want to eat at that time, the beauty of this diet being that you can eat as much popcorn as you can hold. And if you pop it without grease and eat it without salt, you can shave a few inches off the old spare tire in no time at all.

How much weight can you lose on my fabulous popcorn diet? As much as 100 pounds a month—that is, if you start out weighing 2,000 pounds!

Seriously, though, folks, I have lost as much as 35 pounds dieting in about two months. But all that weight loss cannot be attributed to a steady diet of popcorn. You see, man cannot live by popcorn alone. He must also take the right kind of vitamin and mineral supplements to fulfill his daily nutritional requirements.

So, during the two months following this past season, when I dropped from 198 to 163 pounds, I spent only the first two weeks of that time on my popcorn diet. I, myself, prefer Orville Redenbacher's® Gourmet® Popping Corn. So, for those first two weeks, it was just Orville and me.

But you might want to supplement this diet of popcorn with some fruit and an occasional veggie or two—right from the beginning. The second 2-4 weeks of my diets, I eat a lot of fresh fruits and vegetables, exclusively.

Then, after I have lost the amount of weight I want to lose, I try to maintain my desired weight by switching to what I call my "F&F, W&W diet." That is, I eat only *fish* and *fowl*, prepared in calorie-conscious ways, and I drink only *water* and *wine* (mostly white wines, which are lower in calories).

Of course, I still pig out occasionally. And during the basketball season, when we are all eating on the run so much, we eat a ton of fast food, so, no matter how much I try, my weight will typically climb right back up there again. Then, in the spring and summer, after I finish the Wolfpack Tour, I go back on my popcorn diet again.

You know, fans talk a lot about the training table. But if the truth were known, folks, basketball players—and coaches—spend more time in fast-food places than anywhere else.

And while I happen to love *all* fast-food restaurants, a steady diet of burgers and fried chicken with French fries and milkshakes will have me looking like the Pillsbury Dough Boy again in no time flat. So when I'm counting my calories, I try to stick to light and tasty meals.

One of the few places where I can get this type of meal on the road is a new chain of "lite" fast-food restaurants called D'Lites, which features the fast-food staples such as hamburgers, chicken and fish, salad bar and stuffed baked potatoes—all prepared for the diet-conscious consumer. The emphasis on more nutrition and fewer calories is obvious throughout the menu, which features frozen-yogurt desserts and lite wines and beers, among other items.

So, whenever I'm in the mood for a quick, light lunch or supper, I just slip on the old Nikes and slide over to the D'Lites on North Boulevard in Raleigh.

But enough of this discourse on dieting and diet foods. Everyone has his or her own method. Just choose the one that works for you, eat moderately and wisely, exercise regularly and you should lead a longer, happier life.

And always, always remember what my favorite Muppet, Miss Piggy, has to say on the subject of pigging out: "Never eat more than you can lift."

NEVER SAY NEVER

It is almost midnight, on a cold night in December 1978, and I am riding with *New York Times* reporter Tony Kornheiser, who is quizzing me about the secrets behind the success of my Iona College team, which had literally come from nowhere when I got there, in 1976, to be ranked as high as ninth nationally in preseason polls at the start of my fourth season with the Gaels.

Two of the players who have propelled us into the limelight are a flashy guard named Glenn Vickers and a blue-chip center named Jeff Ruland.

Tony is driving and we have just stopped at a light, when a car carrying Glenn zips through the red light. "There goes Vick," I say. "Must be a study break."

Then Jeff Ruland pulls up alongside us, and we banter back and forth good-naturedly.

I am laughing so hard that it's bringing tears to my eyes. Tony is pointing out that my contract with Iona expires in August and I have had offers from a number of other schools in the past year. He asks, Have I ever thought about coaching at one of those big-time basketball schools down South.

Sure, I had thought about it. But my question I asked myself was, Would my "act" play down South? I think the results are in on that one.

People are always asking me if I ever experienced any "culture shock" when I moved down here. Sure, this Italian kid from Queens had some adjusting to do, coming from a megametropolis like New York City and settling in Raleigh. But I'll tell you what, I found when I came here that there are more similarities than differences between the people I grew up with in the urban North and the people of the Research Triangle area. Both there and here, I see the same focus on family and the very real concern for people.

We may not *sound* alike. On Sundays, I may have eaten raviolis at two o'clock, and Southerners had something else. But the care for each other and the friendliness and warmth and the family attitude is very strong, both in Corona — the Italian part of Queens where I grew up — and where I live now.

We're going on five years here now—I mean, you call up my house and my kids, Nicole, Jamie and Lee Ann, are going to say, "Hey." And it's "Y'all this" and Jamie sounds like she was born and raised here. I mean, if there's anybody who talks more Southern than Jamie Jill Valvano, I haven't met 'em yet.

Pam and I—we'll never change the way we talk, because that's too ingrained. The children—if you listen to my three kids talk, you would think "There's no question about where they're from." And the baby really is from here. I mean, she's lived here since right after she was born.

I have talked about my dreams before. One of my childhood dreams was to grow up to coach the New York Knicks. I no longer have that dream, and right now I just can't imagine ever leaving Raleigh.

I will tell you this: Pam says that if I decide to leave the area, I will be going without her and the kids. I cannot think of a job or an offer that would make me want to leave North Carolina State University—because we are *happy* here. I cannot say, categorically, that I would *never* leave North Carolina. I never say never. But I can say this: I am a firm believer in that old Italian proverb, "You don't mess with happy."

INDEX

ABOUT THE AUTHOR

James Thomas Valvano has been described by a New York newspaper columnist as a man who could sell falsies to Dolly Parton! But he assures us that that is just not true. (And, anyway, his lovely wife Pam would not even let him try.)

The second of three sons of Rocco and Angelina Valvano, Jim was born March 10, 1946 in Queens, N.Y., where he lived until 1959, when his family moved to Seaford, Long Island. While in high school, Jim earned 10 varsity letters in three sports, performing as a shortstop on the baseball team, a guard on the basketball team and quarterback on the football team. He captained all three teams his senior year. And he was also the only athlete in Seaford High School's history to earn all-league honors in three sports the same year (1962-63).

In the fall of 1963, Jim enrolled at his father's alma mater, Rutgers University; and played one year of freshman basketball and three years of varsity basketball in Coach Bill Foster's program, co-captaining the Scarlet Knights his senior year and leading the team to a third-place finish in the National Invitational Tournament.

After graduation with a B.A. in English/education, Jim stayed at Rutgers as an assistant coach under Bill Foster for the 1968 and 1969 seasons, was head coach at Johns Hopkins University in Baltimore for the 1970 season, and was then an assistant to Coach Dee Rowe at the University of Connecticut in Storrs for the next three seasons.

In 1973 Jim became head coach at Bucknell University in Lewisburg, Pa., and in 1976 he became head basketball coach at Iona College in New Rochelle, N.Y. In five seasons there, he posted a 96-47 won-lost record and took the Gaels to two NCAA tournaments.

Jim Valvano was named head coach at North Carolina State University in March 1980, and since then has piled up 81 victories—including a 54-52 win over the University of Houston for the 1983 National Championship—against 47 defeats.

In 1983 he was named Coach-of-the-Year by the Hawkeye Rebounders Club of Cedar Rapids, Iowa; by Medalist Sports Industries of St. Louis, Mo.; by Spalding Sporting Goods Company; and by *Eastern Basketball* magazine.

And Jim was recently named to the first *Esquire Register* of "Men and Women Under Forty Who Are Changing America."

A lifetime member of the Wolfpack Club, Jim Valvano lives in Cary with his wife, the former Pamela Sue Levine of Seaford, N.Y., and their three daughters: Nicole, 15; Jamie, 12; and Lee Ann, 4.

Jim's first book, *Too Soon to Quit: The Story of N.C. State's 1983 Championship Season*, was a local best-seller, which *Durham Sun* sports editor Frank Dascenzo called "an excellent package of drama (and) heart-warming stories. It'll live only forever."